MW01280166

ESSENTIAL LIFE SKILLS FOR TEENS

13 DIFFERENT WAYS TO USE YOUR CRITICAL THINKING, MANAGE YOUR TIME BETTER, SET YOUR SMART GOALS, AND NAVIGATE SOCIAL MEDIA SAFELY

DAVID SKIDDY

Copyright © 2022 David Skiddy. All rights reserved.

The content contained within this book may not be reproduced, duplicated, or transmitted without direct written permission from the author or the publisher.

Under no circumstances will any blame or legal responsibility be held against the publisher, or author, for any damages, reparation, or monetary loss due to the information contained within this book, either directly or indirectly.

Legal Notice:

This book is copyright protected. It is only for personal use. You cannot amend, distribute, sell, use, quote, or paraphrase any part, or the content within this book, without the consent of the author or publisher.

Disclaimer Notice:

Please note the information contained within this document is for educational and entertainment purposes only. All effort has been executed to present accurate, up-to-date, reliable, and complete information. No warranties of any kind are declared or implied. Readers acknowledge that the author is not engaged in the rendering of legal, financial, medical, or professional advice. The content within this book has been derived from various sources. Please consult a licensed professional before attempting any techniques outlined in this book.

By reading this document, the reader agrees that under no circumstances is the author responsible for any losses, direct or indirect, that are incurred as a result of the use of the information contained within this document, including, but not limited to, errors, omissions, or inaccuracies.

CONTENTS

A GIFT TO OUR READERS

The purchase of this book includes goal setting, time
management and budget worksheets.
Let's start working on it.
Please scan QR code
Or visit
Davidskiddy.com
To let us know where to deliver it to

HOW ESSENTIAL LIFE SKILLS FOR TEENS WAS BORN

The teenage years mark the advent of adulthood. It is a stage of life where you must make critical decisions that will dictate how your adult life will turn out to be. As a result, there are many things you have to consider in order to ensure that you are making the best use of your time as a teenager—including learning and developing important life skills.

Developing life skills is a continuous process of improvement. It is a process that starts when one is a baby and then carries on for the rest of one's life. Some skills we are taught, and some we learn organically, without noticing it. Some skills we learn by observing other people, while other skills must be learned and practiced.

Any skill in your life can be considered a life skill. For example, tying shoelaces, swimming, driving, and using a computer are all useful life skills for most people. But, broadly speaking, the term "life skills" is often used to describe skills that help us effectively and adequately deal with life's challenges.

This book was born out of my desire to ensure that all teenagers have access to guidance that will help them maximize their potential and translate it into a fulfilling life. It contains life skills that I wished I'd known about as a teenager. It is an attempt to help you activate your better self and actualize your dreams as early in life as possible.

By learning the life skills outlined in this book, you will increase your understanding of the world around you, equip yourself with the tools you need to lead a more productive and fulfilling life, and find ways to deal with the challenges that life will inevitably bring to you.

INTRODUCTION

In his Sophomore year in high school, Sanil Chawla decided to follow his passion—Web Development—by launching a startup. But being under 18, he discovered that there was too much red tape that made it impossible for him to file the legal paperwork to start a company.

Rather than giving up on his dreams or pushing them aside till 'later', Sanil started researching ways to lower the barrier for teenagers interested in entrepreneurship. That was when he discovered fiscal sponsorship, which allows non-profits to extend their legal status and support to small scale organizations with similar missions.

Seeing this as an opportunity, Sanil developed software that automates the legal paperwork for small companies, creating a scalable version of fiscal sponsorship. This led to the creation of Hack+, a non-profit that provides sponsorship to student-founded charities. Over the years, Hack+ has received sponsorship, funding, and other forms of support from big companies like Microsoft, Google, Amazon, and many others. Hack+ has helped launch over 100 organizations worldwide and continues to support both profit and non-profit organizations and startups. To this day, Sanil continues to apply the life skills he learned early in his teenage life and still serves as the CEO of his first company, which now operates under the name Slingshot.

Stories like that of Sanil are not hard to come by; there are many people around the world who develop the right life skills early on in life and go on to apply them well into adulthood, too. We've all heard such success stories. The important thing to note here is that most successful people start working on their skills when they're still teenagers.

It's no coincidence that the teenage years are thought to be one of the most essential periods of our lives. It's a formative stage that often indicates what our adulthood will turn out to be like. However, as important a life stage as it is, it's also a confusing one. It's a bridge between being a child and being a grown-up. As a teenager, you feel like you're old enough to be on your own; at the same time, however, you need love, care, attention, and understanding from your parent-figures. You want to make decisions on your own, but you also need guidance. It's a delicate balance that needs to be achieved— and it's not always easy. But no matter your circumstances, you have the power to control how well you prepare yourself for the next stage of your life.

As a teenager, you begin to extend your relationship with others beyond parents and family; your peers and the outside world suddenly become major influences in your life. From social media to real-life peer group activities, you become exposed to new forces of influence that can change how you see yourself or the world around you.

You also start to think more like a grown-up, and your mental processes become more analytical. You can now think abstractly, express yourself better, and develop independent thought processes. These teenage years are the years of creativity, idealism, vitality, and adventure. They are also the years of experimentation and making decisions on key issues—especially those related to your physical body and sex. Therefore, the teenage stage is a turning point in life, a period of increased potential, and at the same time a more vulnerable period.

Some of the key issues and concerns observed in teenage years include issues related to forming self-image, managing emotions, building relationships, strengthening social skills, and coping with, or resisting, peer pressure. Teens are more susceptible to high-risk situations–and more likely to succumb to them. Some young people can deal with these challenges effectively, while others may struggle. How you deal with these problems depends on many factors, including your personality, psychosocial support from your environment (including parents, teachers, and peers), and the life skills you possess–which is why such skills are so important.

Life skills are effective tools that allow you, as an adolescent, to act responsibly, take initiative, and take control of situations you might find yourself in. The World Health Organization (WHO) defines life skills as "abilities for adaptive and positive behavior that enable individuals to deal effectively with the demands and challenges of everyday life." When you are adaptive and positive in the face of a challenge, this means that you can adjust your behavior as needed in order to effectively overcome it, and that you remain forward-looking and hopeful in your ability to find solutions even in difficult situations.

If you're wondering what life skills you should be developing as a teenager, the answer is that there are several. Broadly speaking, life skills include psychosocial and interpersonal skills, which can help you make wise decisions, communicate effectively, solve problems, and think critically and creatively. These life skills will also help you manage your own life, build healthy relationships, empathize with others, and stay healthy and productive.

As a teenager, you want to hang out with friends, have fun, and enjoy your adolescence. Working on developing your life skills may be the last thing on your mind. This, in itself, is neither strange nor inherently bad. In fact, social interactions are indeed helpful for some important life skills.

However, to lead a successful and healthy life and to over-come the challenges that lie ahead, it is very important to find a good balance between having fun and preparing for the future. And since schools often fail to teach teenagers essential life skills such as critical thinking, time manage-ment, and financial management (among others), you must learn these basic skills by yourself–and the sooner you start, the better. But, since you are reading this book, you probably know that already.

So, let's get started!

1

IF YOU CAN THINK IT, YOU CAN DO IT

When Sanil Chawla discovered the problems associated with registering a company as a teenager, the easiest path for him would have been to wait till he was over 18. However, Sanil is not the type to give up on his dreams. So, he set out to look for ways to bypass these bottlenecks and get his company registered. He exhibited two solid and essential life skills in that situation: creative thinking and critical thinking.

CRITICAL THINKING

If you use a search engine to look up the meaning of critical thinking, you will be surprised to find that there is no agreed upon definition. Broadly speaking, however, critical thinking refers to one's ability to look at a situation as thoroughly as possible and make a sound evaluation. That generally translates into better and more informed decision-making.

Critical thinking is a highly essential skill–and it's one you're already using in your daily life. You use it every time you buy something online or at the mall, plan your time, or make your 'to-do list.' You also use critical thinking every time you evaluate information from the news, blogs, or online articles.

So how does critical thinking work exactly? Let's say, for example, that you want to buy a pair of shoes. First, you start thinking about what kind of shoes you want (sandals, trainers, high heels, boots, etc.). What do you need the shoes for? Do they need to serve a specific purpose (like running shoes, for example) or do you just need them to complete a look you hand in mind? Once you decide on the kind of shoes you want, you start comparing the prices on a couple of platforms; you think about the materials the shoes you like are made of and compare them to some alternatives based on how long you expect them to last. You might also check how quickly the shoes will be delivered. These are all examples of critical thinking. How deep you will 'dig' before you make a decision depends on how big of a decision it is, and how important the problem you're trying to solve is.

Critical thinking is an ability that helps you evaluate information, be curious, look for evidence, and approach things with skepticism. It is an essential part of problem-solving, goal setting, and decision-making. Regardless of what you want to do later in your life–study, work or take a gap year–there will be a point where you have to make a decision. At that point in time, your critical thinking skill will come into play in a significant way.

So, let's go back to Sanil for a moment. How did he apply critical thinking to his situation? After discovering that he was having issues with the registration of his company, Sanil did what most of his peers would probably not have considered. Instead of letting the obstacle he encountered stop him, he thought of how he could bypass it. He accepted the presence of the problem, and then thought about how he could solve it. In short, he put his research and critical thinking skills to work. To understand his process a little bit better, let's take a closer look at the components of critical thinking.

The Six Sub-Components of Critical Thinking

We can divide critical thinking into six sub-components, outlined below.

1. Identification

The first element of critical thinking is identifying the situation or problem and the factors that might affect it. Once you clearly understand the situation and the people, groups, or factors that affect it or are affected by it, you can study the problem and its potential solutions in more depth. In the case of Sanil, he discovered that, when it comes to registering a company, people younger than 18 are at a disadvantage; they are simply unable to file the paperwork they need. He identified the problem (difficulty filing paperwork) and the people affected by it (teenagers under 18). With this information at hand, he was then able to start thinking about a solution.

How to improve: When encountering any new situation, problem or scenario, stop and take a mental inventory of the situation and ask the following questions:

- *Who is involved in this problem/situation?*
- *What are they trying to achieve?*
- *What are the problems they are encountering?*

2. Research

When comparing arguments on a specific issue, independent research ability is essential. Viewpoints are meant to be persuasive; this means that facts and data in their favor may lack context or come from problematic sources. You can solve this problem by verifying independently, finding sources of information and evaluating them. That was how Sanil found the solution he was looking for, Hack+. He did research to see if there was another option for registering a company as a minor. He gathered information and thought about how what he was learning could be best applied to solve the problem he was facing.

How to improve: Paying attention to claims without sources may help. Is the person presenting the argument providing information on where they obtained this information? If you ask for a source of information or try to find it yourself and there is no clear answer, that's a red flag. It is also crucial to know that not all sources are equally valid; take the time to understand the difference between academic and non-academic articles.

3. Recognizing Bias

This skill can be challenging because even the smartest among us may sometimes fail to recognize bias, as it can be easily perceived as a preference. Critical thinkers will do their best to evaluate information objectively. Think of yourself as a judge: you want to assess the arguments of all parties, while bearing in mind the prejudices that each party may have. Learning to discard your own personal biases influencing your judgment is equally essential, and it may be even more difficult.

How to improve: First, you must be aware of biases. When evaluating information or arguments, ask yourself the following questions:

- *Who is this good for?*
- *Does the source of this information have an agenda?*
- *Does the source ignore or omit information that does not support its claims?*
- *Is the source using emotive language to manipulate people's perception of the information?*

4. Inference

Reasoning and drawing conclusions based on the information provided to you are key for mastering critical thinking. Reports are not always accompanied by a summary explaining their meaning. Instead, you usually need to evaluate the information provided and draw conclusions based on the original data.

We do this exercise every day without even realizing it. Say, for example, that you got to school and cannot find your math homework. You then remember that you weren't able to finish it the previous night and that you decided to finish it in the morning. However, you overslept and left the house in a hurry. From the information you remembered, you can draw the conclusion that you probably left it on your desk back at home.

Inference capabilities allow you to discover possible results when evaluating scenarios. However, it is also essential to note that not all inferences are correct. For example, if you hear that someone weighs 280 pounds, you might infer that they are overweight or unhealthy. However, other data like height and body composition might show that your conclusion was wrong. For instance, that person might be a bodybuilder, which means that his body mass is mostly muscle.

How to improve: Inferring is the same as making an educated guess. Before concluding, you can consciously collect as much information as possible to enhance your ability to make correct inferences. For example, when faced with new information to evaluate, first try to browse through clues that appear in your sources—such as titles, images, and prominent statistics—and then explicitly ask yourself what *you* think is happening.

5. Determining Relevance

One of the most challenging parts of critical thinking is to find the right information to consider. In many cases, you will find information that seems essential, but upon further investigation is not.

How to improve: The best way to better determine relevance is to establish a clear direction based on what you are trying to figure out. For example, is your task to find a solution? Should you determine the trend? Once you have determined your goal, you can use it to determine what is relevant.

However, even with clear goals, determining what information is genuinely relevant can still be challenging. Making a physical list of data points in order of relevance could help to solve this problem. If you do this, you will probably end up with a list containing relevant information at the top and some information at the bottom that you can overlook. You can then focus on the information in the middle of the list to decide whether they belong in the "relevant" section or whether they can be ignored.

6. Curiosity

Accepting the surface value of everything presented to you is easy, but when faced with a situation that requires critical thinking, lack of curiosity can have disastrous effects. And even though curiosity comes naturally to us when we are younger, it's a trait that we need to put some effort in maintaining because, as you get older, curiosity can fade away.

How to improve: While it may seem like curiosity is something you're born with, you can train yourself to make use of that curiosity productively. Made a conscious effort to ask open-ended questions about things that you witness daily. When you cultivate that habit, you can then follow up on the questions and validate answers.

These are the six sub-components to critical thinking, and Sanil had to go through all of them—either consciously or otherwise. Through this process, he was able to find an effective solution to the problem he identified.

The Importance and Benefits of Critical Thinking

There are a lot of benefits that you'll get from developing your critical thinking abilities. Let's look at some of them below.

▷ It Helps You Improve Your Language and Presentation Skills

To best express yourself, you will need to learn how to think clearly and systematically, i.e., you have to practice the art to master the craft. Critical thinking also means knowing how to break down texts in order to comprehend them on a deeper level.

▷ It Helps Your Creativity

By practicing critical thinking, you are teaching yourself to solve problems and develop new and creative ideas. Moreover, critical thinking will help you understand how to adjust and adapt these creative ideas in response to any given problem or situation. That explains, in part, how Sanil was able to find such a creative solution to his problem.

▷ It Is Important for Your Success in Life

Critical thinking is vital regardless of what you choose to do in life. So even if you are not planning to start a company like Sanil, you must know that critical thinking is essential for all aspects of your life. According to the World Economic Forum, critical thinking is one of the top desired skills worldwide. It helps you analyze information and pushes you to think outside the box, develop innovative solutions to problems, and develop systematic plans.

▷ It Helps Improve Decision-Making

Critical thinking will help you deal with your everyday problems as you face them. After practicing critical thinking for a while, it will become something that you do subconsciously, and it will guide your decision-making process. It will help you think independently and trust your gut feeling more than ever.

▷ It Improves the Quality of Your Relationships

Critical thinking will enable you to understand others' perspectives better and help you become more open-minded and tolerant of the views of others. It will allow you to view your relationships more objectively, and to avoid rushing to conclusions about other people's behavior.

Critical Thinking Vs. Overthinking

At this point it's important to point out that critical thinking is not the same as overthinking. It is not uncommon for people to mix them up, but the truth is that they are as different as day is from night. Overthinking usually means that you obsess over a subject or situation. You find yourself stuck, the same thoughts and scenarios playing out it out in your head over and over again. An example of overthinking is this: you ask a question in class about an assignment and then start doubting whether you were right to do so. "I shouldn't have asked that question in class. Now everyone thinks I'm stupid." You replay the situation in your head, again and again. You keep asking questions like, "Why couldn't I just have kept my mouth shut?" "Were people making fun of me for asking that?" That is overthinking.

Instead of thinking like that, you need to approach the situation from a critical thinking perspective. The problem was that you didn't have enough information to complete the assignment. Wanting to do well in your assignment, you let your curiosity guide you towards the additional information you needed in order to achieve your goal, and you asked a question.

The difference between critical thinking and overthinking is evident. With critical thinking, you accept the problem and understand what needs to be done in order to solve it. With overthinking, your mind is scattered; the more you think of the situation, the more you lose sight of it. Finally, you end up focusing on a million things that have nothing to do with the initial problem you encountered, and you spend your time judging and second-guessing your solution instead of benefiting from it.

Critical thinking serves to help you assimilate a situation, understand it better, and make excellent decisions. It is a productive and admirable skill set for you as a teenager (or anybody for that matter), while overthinking is counterproductive (or outrightly destructive).

CREATIVE THINKING

Creative thinking is a close kin of critical thinking. These two life skills go hand-in-hand and complement each other. While critical thinking helps you shed light on a problem and enhances how you understand it, creative thinking enables you to see solutions that many would not see. In short, creative thinking is all about "thinking outside the box."

A sentence that I've heard many times from people concerning creative thinking is, "I'm not art-inclined, so I can't be creative." If you're one of these people, hold your thoughts for a moment. Let's go back to the story of Sanil for a moment.

The problem he had initially was that he couldn't register his web design business because he was too young to file all the necessary paperwork. However, this problem led him to create a solution that allows teenagers to register their business regardless of age. How did he do it? Creative thinking. He thought outside the box.

His critical thinking helped him understand the problem, but it was his creative thinking that pushed him to consider such an innovative solution. An otherwise overlooked problem for entrepreneurial teenagers was no longer an issue, and it was all because Sanil was able to combine his critical and creative thinking skills.

And you can do it too! You can think creatively and provide innovative solutions to whatever problem you might have.

Is Creative Thinking Learned Or Inherited?

The question of whether creative thinking is learned or inherited has no simple answer. Creativity is indeed inherited, but it can also be developed over time. In fact, even if you are naturally very creative, you still need to foster your creativity on a regular basis for it to shine.

So, before you write yourself off as someone who could never be creative,, know that you can develop your creativity and your creative thinking skills if you decide to do so. The question that then naturally comes up is, "How can I develop my creative thinking skills?" Let's look at the answer next.

10+1 Steps to Developing Your Creative Thinking Skills With Confidence

1. Absorb Different Types of Content

If you diversify the types of content you consume daily, your creative thinking skills will benefit greatly. After all, the information you absorb can be combined, remixed, and reused in many ways to provide solutions. However, if you don't incorporate diversity, this will become impossible.

To diversify your content consumption, you can take advantage of the vast selection of content types on the Internet. After all, we are in an internet-powered world. Try to access different blogs, YouTube channels, and social media profiles that you are not used to, preferably those dealing with topics you don't engage with frequently.

If you like science, go the opposite direction and find some art material. Art and science are an excellent mix. Coming up with new ideas is like trying to create a new color; you can't create green unless you mix yellow and blue.

This also applies to using different media types, such as text, video, audio, and even more specific media, such as ebooks, podcasts, infographics, etc. So, for example, if you are a passionate reader of ebooks, you can start listening to podcasts more often.

2. Create Daily

If you have a weight loss goal, you will most likely design an exercise plan that requires daily effort and commitment. That same concept applies to the development of your creative thinking skills. With that in mind, make sure to try to create new things every day. It does not have to be significant or essential as long as it is something new derived from the content you are absorbing. Draw a flower in your sketchbook. When you're out for a walk, use your phone to snap some pictures—not selfies, but pictures of a flower, house, or fence. Look carefully, and maybe something will catch your eye. If this is not an option for you, you can try writing a poem in your diary.

These daily creations can also serve as solutions to everyday problems faced by you or your community. For example, if there is an elderly person in your neighborhood, why not create an online group to help organize the community to provide assistance to your elderly neighbor? The essential part of this process is developing the habit of using your creativity as often as possible.

3. Build a Network of Creative Thinkers

You might have heard the saying, "show me your friends and I'll tell you who you are." To become more creative, include creative people in your social circle. Working with creative people gives you new ideas and opportunities–and it can be great fun, too!

Integrating with peers is a great way to exercise creativity. However, be careful not to let your thoughts and innovations be so influenced by others that they become the same as everyone else's. When creating this network, seek as much diversity as possible, as diversity is extremely beneficial to developing your creative thinking.

An easy way to build a network of creative thinkers is to look for creative groups on social platforms. You can also check if there are any creative classes taking place at your high school. If nothing interests you there, then check what your town has to offer regarding youth clubs. Finally, if you can't find any interest group, use your critical thinking skills and start one yourself!

4. Become an Expert

One of the best ways to understand, cultivate, and develop creativity is to become an expert in your chosen field or subject matter. With a rich understanding of a subject, you will become better at coming up with new and innovative solutions to problems.

Choose an activity that you love. For example, if you have always been interested in the sky, stars, and the planets, follow your passion and dive deep into astronomy. Or, if you have always wanted to learn dancing or baking, then take the time to do just that!

5. Reward Your Curiosity

Many people feel that indulging in curiosity is a distraction, and they try to suppress it, suppressing their creativity along the way. When you are curious about something, feel free to indulge. Learn to explore new topics and discover new interests.

6. Be Adventurous

When developing your creative skills, you need to be willing to take risks to improve your abilities. Although your efforts may not lead to success every time, you will still enhance your creative talents and develop skills that will serve you in the future. Go to a movie without friends and give yourself the opportunity and space to develop your own thoughts about what the movie is about, what you liked or what you disliked about it. Write a message to your future self; put it into the bottle and don't open it for a couple of years.

7. Build Your Confidence

Insecurity or lack of trust in your abilities inhibits creativity. Therefore, you must build up your confidence if you want to develop your creative thinking skills. The more confident you are, the freer you will feel about expressing your ideas. Therefore, pay attention to your progress, praise your efforts, and always look for ways to reward your creativity. You need to understand that confidence comes with experience. The more you practice, the better you will become. Get more experience and you'll see your confidence levels grow.

8. Fight the Fear of Failure

Worrying that you might make mistakes or fail in your efforts will hinder your progress. Whenever you find yourself feeling this way, remind yourself that mistakes are only part of the process. Although you may occasionally stumble on the road to creativity, you will eventually achieve your goals. No one has achieved great things without making mistakes. Some people experience greater levels of failure than others, but no matter how many times you fail, it shouldn't put you off trying again. Instead, it should encourage you to use your critical thinking skills. Identify why you or your plan hasn't succeeded, gather additional information if needed, adjust your strategy and go again.

9. Explore Multiple Solutions

Next time you solve a problem, try not to settle on a single solution. Instead, try to develop various solutions. Rather than simply adopting your first idea, take the time to consider other possible ways to deal with this situation. Doing that will put your brain in a position where it automatically tries to solve problems in many different ways, thereby sharpening your creative thinking skill.

10. Keep a Creativity Diary

Start keeping a diary to track your creative process and keep track of the ideas you generate. A log is a great way to reflect on your achievements and find other possible solutions. In addition, this diary can save ideas, which you can use as a source of inspiration in the future.

11. Challenge Yourself and Create Opportunities

Once you have mastered the essential creative thinking skills, you must continue to challenge yourself to improve your ability further. Find more complex methods, try new things, and avoid always using the exact solutions as in the past. Besides challenging yourself, you also need to create opportunities for yourself. This may involve working on new projects or finding new tools to use in current projects.

Sources of Inspiration

Never expect creativity to just happen. That goes for everything you do in life. Things don't happen because you want them to happen. They happen because you made them happen. To make creativity happen for you, look for new sources of inspiration; they will bring you fresh ideas and inspire you to produce unique solutions to problems. For example, read a new book, visit a new place, listen to new music, or have a lively debate with friends. Use the strategy or technique that works best for you.

All these techniques above will help you develop your creative thinking skills. In essence, creative thinking skills can be learned and developed. When you develop these skills and use them, you will create unique solutions, just like Sanil did.

It all starts with you. Have the desire to develop these skills and take necessary steps towards your goal. Start slowly and build up the skills with consistency–consistency is vital. Teach yourself a new skill, explore topics you're interested in, play brain games like sudoku, crosswords, or learn a new language. Create a story, form a mental picture, and never stop asking what, why, when, what if, etc. Be a continuous learner and be open-minded. Creativity is a muscle, and muscles need to be trained.

At the end of this book, I've included links to websites where you can find different brain games and brain training website recommendations. But first, let's explore the rest of the essential life skills you should aim to develop.

2

PROBLEMS SUCK! SOLUTIONS ROCK!

P roblems exist and will always exist—know this and know peace! But the beautiful thing about most problems is that there are solutions for them, and finding solutions is extremely gratifying. It's like getting an A+ in an important exam. That is why you need to have problem-solving skills as a teenager. It will help grow your confidence and it will help you improve your life and the lives of others.

Imagine yourself in this everyday situation: you have an essential task to attend to–this could be schoolwork or even a self-assigned task. Aside from this task, you have your after-school work and also need to help a friend with something you had previously agreed to help them with. Here's the problem: you have only 5 hours to do all of this. Deep in your mind, you know that even if you could somehow split yourself in two, it would still be hard to do everything within that time frame. Yet, you have to make sure everything gets done. The process of finding a way around this issue is called "problem-solving."

If you successfully attend to all of these tasks, it will make you feel confident about taking on even more daunting tasks in the future. Imagine how Sanil must have felt after finding a solution to the daunting problem he was faced with; suddenly, the sky was the limit!

When it comes to creating solutions and making difficult decisions, we love to make plans–and we make a whole lot of them. We do that because we want the perfect plan, and to make excellent plans, we have to understand what the problem is and exactly what the process of solving it looks like.

However, this can take a very long time, and, in the end, we end up focusing on the planning process so much that we drift further and further away from actually doing something that helps us reach our goal. We overthink. and get stuck in the decision-making process. But the truth is that there's no perfect solution or plan for any problem. So instead of focusing on how to get to that perfect solution, focus on a solution. YOUR SOLUTION!

Action is better than no action; The way you do what you do when you have a problem is not important. What's important is that you take the necessary step towards finding a solution to the problem. Smart teenagers like you should know that to solve any problem, the goal is to try out solutions, analyze the feedback you get, and adjust your solutions accordingly, until you get the result you want.

FOUR TYPES OF PROBLEMS WE ENCOUNTER EVERY DAY

In 1999, while working at IBM, Dave Snowden came up with a way of looking at problems to help people understand what they faced and what solutions they should look for. Let's look at some of his observations about the different types of problems we are most commonly faced with.

1. Simple Problems

According to Snowden's framework, the first category of problems includes problems of a simple nature. Simple problems are those that have been previously solved, and an effective solution has been established. Once you have determined that a problem is simple, you can approach it with a previously tried-and-tested method.

For example, you left a tube of ice cream on the table. As a result of you forgetting to put it in the freezer, it has melted. The problem is that it's now inedible. The solution to never having your ice cream melt again? Just keep it in the freezer from now on.

2. Complicated Problems

This is a known yet unknown problem. That statement seems complicated, right? Well, so are these kinds of problems. Complicated problems are problems for which solutions exist, even if you are not personally familiar with them.

For those who have enough knowledge, figuring out these problems is possible. So even if you don't know enough on the subject yourself, you know that people are dedicated to solving these exact problems. So, when faced with them, you turn to these dedicated problem-solvers for the solution instead of spending unnecessary time trying to find the answer.

Think of this; you're driving your car, and it's making strange noises. You get worried and wonder what the problem could be. Of course, if you know about the workings of a vehicle, you can easily spot the problem and fix it yourself. But, if you don't know how to find the solution, you can be sure that a mechanic will know the problem and solve it. In that case, the simple answer to this known yet unknown problem is to call a mechanic.

3. Complex Problems

The third class of problems includes complex problems. Like complicated problems, their cause and effect are not obvious to everyone, like they are for simple problems and the ice cream example we looked at before.

The difference between complicated problems and complex problems is that complex problems are problems that others don't know exist, and as a result no known solutions exist, either. These are problems you discover when you take an action and find yourself in unknown territory. You must try and find your own solution, trying and testing it as you go. This is the sort of problem that Sanil encountered when he tried to register his company as a teenager.

We can further explore complex problems with the example of Twitch, a streaming network that allows people to play video games while streaming so that others can watch them play. Like Sanil's Hack+, this is not a product that's an obvious solution to a problem, unless you look at it in retrospect. But Twitch is an incredible success story. Amazon bought it in 2014 for US$970 million.

The company's first product idea was a calendar integrated with Gmail. Of course, Google later launched Google Calendar, essentially forcing the company to change lanes. Their new idea? Live broadcasting.

At first, one of the founders decided to live broadcast his life 24/7. He and his team established a high-speed live broadcast service that many people could use simultaneously and, with a camera on his head and a large backpack with a computer in it, he began broadcasting. But it turns out that no one wanted to watch that live broadcast.

So they opened up the idea. Maybe people want to broadcast themselves live? But, unfortunately, this iteration of the concept also did not work, and they ran out of funds. Then, they discovered that people were watching live streams of others playing video games.

They capitalized on this discovery, and it turned out that a group of avid fans and casual gamers really wanted to watch live as top players played video games. Fast forward to today, and people can make a fortune by playing video games and live streaming it for others to watch.

This is an extreme example of solving a need that no one realizes exists or is trying to solve. But the problems you'll face as a teenager trying to navigate your teenage years and beyond can sometimes be tricky, too, with no obvious solution.

So what you should do when faced with unique, complex problems is try something and see what happens. Get results and adjust what you are doing. Then try again. Adjust again. Conduct a series of small experiments and let the solution surface.

4. Chaotic Problems

The fourth category of problems Dave Snowden identified includes what he refers to as chaotic problems. These essentially refer to a crisis—one that most probably affects not only you, but a lot of people at once.

For example, suppose there is a protest in your school that turns into a riot. What you need to do is such a scenario is to quickly take steps to encapsulate the problem, define its boundaries, and scale it down. Speed is vital for solving this kind of problem. If you delay the decision-making process for chaotic issues, they will only worsen with time.

So let's go back to our example. Suppose a scream is heard from one side of the school protest, and the situation becomes chaotic. Everyone starts running around not knowing what to do; they transcend from being a group of individuals into a group of thugs. What do you do?

First, don't panic. I cannot emphasize how important this is. Blind fear makes people get trampled and killed. What you need to do is take this chaotic problem and see it as a complex one. Breathe; take a minute to assess the situation and your options. To do so, you must first find an escape route so that you can give yourself freedom to think. When you are just another body tossed around, you can't do anything. But if you can get away from the noise and fear, you can start coming up with a plan.

Again, speed is essential. Once you come up with an idea that could possibly work, give it a go. Try it out, see how it affects the situation, and adjust it as necessary until you find a solution that works.

This method of trial and error may be scary in the moment. But it is also an opportunity to learn and discover new things about yourself and about the world. Chaotic problems can bring about solutions that can then be used to help more people than you ever imagined–just like the solutions developed by other problem-solvers around the world.

Now that you are familiar with the types of problems you might face in your daily life, let's look at how you can develop the problem-solving skills you need to address such problems as a teenager.

Problem-solving involves discovering a problem, carefully analyzing it, and finding solutions to address it. It requires you to take the time to gain a thorough understanding of a situation and to then use your creative and critical thinking skills in a way that helps you move forward.

We all have a natural tendency to avoid difficulties in life, simply because of their unpleasant nature. However, it's important to understand that difficulties are also valuable opportunities for growth and innovation. Let's go back to Sanil for a moment: what if he never encountered the difficulty of setting up his company as a teenager? Hack+ and Slingshot would not have existed, and all the people who have used his services would suffered as a result.

So, instead of running away from the difficulties life throws your way, start seeing them as an opportunity to create solutions–like so many problem-solving teenagers have done before you. It's always better to try and find a solution to a problem than it is to run away from it

FOUR STEPS TO PROBLEM-SOLVING

If problems are an inescapable part of our daily lives, it becomes a no-brainer that you need to learn how to solve them. So let us examine the four steps to solving a problem.

1. Identifying The Problem

The first step to solving a problem is identifying it. After all, you can't address an issue you are not aware of or do not understand. To better understand this, let's look at the story of Kenan Pala.

Kenan always liked to volunteer. He grew up in San Diego, where he would eagerly donate his time to charity kitchens and beach cleanups. To his surprise, however, he discovered that he was excluded from many volunteering activities for causes that he wanted to support, as many non-profit organizations in San Diego don't allow children under 18 to volunteer. Due to the nature of this problem, he realized that it didn't just affect him; it affected a great number of teenagers who wanted to volunteer but–as a result of their age–couldn't do so.

Therefore, in 2017, he founded the non-profit organization Kids4Community–a solution which ensured that any child who wants to volunteer gets the opportunity to do so. Through donations, grants, and charitable activities, Kids4-Community raised $1 million to help alleviate the local homelessness crisis, while engaging over 5,000 young children in voluntary activities.

As you see, the first step Kenan took was to identify the problem. He understood that he could not volunteer for most causes simply because he was underaged. He saw that he was not the only one facing this problem: many potential volunteers were being left out–and that was the problem he identified needed solving and the one which he set out to solve.

2. Planning

This stage is where many people start their problem-solving journey. However, doing so is a big mistake and it's the reason why the majority get stuck at this stage. You can't skip the first step. You have to identify the problem first. Planning can only come after identification, because you can't make a plan unless you know what the plan is for.

This stage is where you'll put your creative and critical thinking skills to work and develop solutions. You need to brainstorm new ideas and consider many different solutions to your problem. This brainstorming process is a common technique in academic and professional environments, but it can also be a powerful tool for cultivating creativity in your daily life.

First, put your judgment and self-criticism aside and start writing down ideas and possible solutions–even if they seem silly, far-fetched, or impossible. This exercise aims to generate as many ideas as possible in a relatively short period. Next, focus on fleshing out your ideas in a little bit more detail; this will help clarify them and it will give you an idea of the ones worth considering in more depth.

Once you have thought up possible solutions to your problem, don't stop there. Instead, consider alternatives and different scenarios. Use "what if..." questions to evaluate solutions based on their effectiveness in various situations. If you adopt a specific approach, what will be the result? By reviewing these alternatives in advance, you will be better able to develop better and more creative solutions to your problems.

After you've come up with a plan and a possible solution to your problem, it's time to take action!

3. Action

Plans up, action down! Without action, there will be no progress. For example, suppose Sanil did not take action after discovering he couldn't set up his company as a teenager. His beautiful solution would never have materialized.

Hack+ and Slingshot are not the result of teenagers not being allowed to set up companies. They are the result of Sanil taking action to solve the problem. The problem would remain if Sanil had not made a plan and acted on it.

The same goes for Kenan Pala and the same goes for you and every other teenage problem-solver like you. Let me put it this way: sleeping doesn't make dreams come true; waking up and taking action do. Therefore, once you've identified your problems and created plans, don't stop there. Get up and act!

4. Check Result

Sanil's solution to the problem he discovered was Hack+. The company covered teenagers who wanted to start non-profit organizations. This solution on its own was excellent. With Hack+, Sanil helped over 900 teenagers and students create their companies and raise millions of dollars from various multinational companies.

Hack+ was making money, and the companies it helped form were doing very well. But Sanil took another essential step. He evaluated the result of the solution he had created. Doing that helped him discover that there's much more to do. Many more solutions can be incorporated within the existing solution.

While he covered non-profits, he saw that for-profit organizations also need to be covered. So he kept evaluating the solution he created and found ways to fine-tune and improve it. Gradually, a more encompassing solution, Slingshot, was created.

After creating solutions to your problems and putting them to work, you have to pay attention to the results generated.

By careful observation, you'll be able to discover other possible and more encompassing solutions or how to make the initial solution even better.

These four steps are proven to work. Many teenagers have used them to make the best of their teenage years and beyond. In case you're wondering how you can apply these steps to your daily life, let's examine a possible scenario.

Suppose you find out that there are quite a few kids in your neighborhood that don't seem to be at school during the day. After asking around, you find out that the reason why they are not at school is that they can't afford tuition. So you've identified the problem.

The next step will be to create a solution. Should you find a way to help these children get scholarship opportunities? Should you campaign for more affordable education in the community? It could be a mix of the two.

Once you've made a plan on how to solve the problem, you then proceed to act. Only then will you have created a solution to the problem. Subsequently, you must evaluate this solution and make better and modified versions that give an even better result. With that, you will have created not only a solution, but a problem-solving champion, too–AND THAT'S YOU!

THREE PROBLEM-SOLVING ACTIVITIES TO TRY

As you begin to build your problem-solving life skills, here are three activities that can help you reach your goal faster. Take time to write these activities in your diary and use them to practice.

Activity 1

Imagine it's been a year since you developed an amazing, innovative solution. What was the problem that you solved? How did you solve it? How has your solution impacted the world? Be as detailed as possible. Then ask yourself: what's keeping you from making it a reality?

Activity 2

Generate ten ideas for solving a particular problem. Then, pick one of the solutions you've thought of and create ten variations of the solution. Finally, pick one of the variations and create another 10 iterations of it. Before you know it, you'd have more than enough solutions for the problem, and you will have trained your brain to come up with solutions much more easily.

Activity 3

Make a game out of problem-solving. When you discover a problem, create rules about how you're going to award yourself points as you go through the problem-solving steps.

Create badges to reward yourself for reaching milestones you've set and create a system for tracking your progress. Doing this will make problem-solving a lot more fun and help you develop problem-solving skills at a faster pace.

3

SET GOALS AND SMASH THEM

When you set goals, you can control the direction of your life. Goals provide you with focus. The decisions and actions you take should bring you closer to achieving these goals. Setting goals can keep you moving forward, increase your happiness, and benefit your life immensely. When you set goals for yourself, you create a vision of your life. Then you start pushing yourself to get the best possible results.

Goals are meant to be smashed–because what is the point of having goals if you don't plan to meet them? But in order to smash your goals, you need to set them first. This is why knowing how to set goals is an essential life skill for any teenager that wants to succeed in life. And this chapter will help you learn how to do just that.

In a soccer match, you need to score as many goals as possible in order to win. Even though luck certainly has a role to play, teams that carefully plan their goals are much more likely to successfully carry them out during the game–and they're much more likely to win! Life operates in a similar way. You need goals to make the best of your life, and you have to plan them correctly to achieve them. And the more you work on your goal-setting skills, the more you will increase your chances of success.

In the story of Sanil that we've been exploring, after discovering that he couldn't register a company due to the fact that he was under 18, he immediately set himself the goal of finding an alternative way to get what he wanted. He found it, and this culminated into a bigger dream–and a bigger goal. He decided to focus his efforts on helping other young people like him to register their own organizations despite the age restriction. That might have looked like a pretty bold goal at the time. But with efficient planning and action, he was able to smash that goal, too! In fact, Slingshot is proof that he never stopped setting more and more ambitious goals for himself. And if you're now wondering if you can be like Sanil, too, then you'll be happy to know that YES, YOU CAN!

A personal goal represents something you want to achieve in life. It can be short-term or long-term. Setting a plan can help you focus more and move towards it; it adds a sense of purpose and direction. In addition, it can help you grow as an individual. But setting goals is not enough; you need steps or systems to achieve them. Goal-setting is a robust process of deciding your ideal future and motivating yourself to turn this vision into reality. By knowing what you want to achieve, you can focus your energy accordingly. And it will also help you be more resilient against disrupting factors that can otherwise easily lead you astray.

WHY DO PEOPLE FAIL TO ACHIEVE THEIR GOALS?

There are many reasons why people might fail to achieve their goals. Let's look at some of those reasons. By exploring them, you'll be able to spot if there's anything on the list that might be presently hindering you from achieving your own goals. You will then be able to take action to remedy them. If you have never set goals before, this list may help you avoid these mistakes and reset your mindset to help you be who you want to be and get where you want to get in life.

▷ **Fear of Success or Failure**

Some people are scared that they will fail or–oddly–that they might succeed. Therefore, they won't even bother to achieve their goals. These people lack confidence in themselves and their potential. In their view, if they fail, everyone will have a negative idea of them. If they succeed, people will have a negative view of them, either out of jealousy or because they think that their success is undeserved. But the truth is that if you trust and believe in yourself, others will do the same. And even though it may sound simple and easy, in reality it can be quite hard. Believing in your potential takes courage and time.

When it comes to fear, fear of failure is understandable. No one likes to fail. It's not a pleasant feeling. But to be scared of success? That sounds a little bit unreal; but it happens. Let me give you an example. About two years ago, I was talking with an old friend. We were discussing life: our plans, failures, and our goals—old and new. It was during our talk that I realized that being afraid of success is indeed possible. My friend explained to me that—even though she hadn't realized this herself until recently—fear of success had stopped her from achieving many great things in her life. She was worried that her family would change their attitude towards her and that she would lose her friends. She was worried about things that she had absolutely no indication were true.

Some people might also think that they are not worthy of achieving their goals. Therefore, they self-sabotage. They miss out on opportunities on purpose, pushing their goals further away instead of moving towards them. People who fall into the trap of self-sabotage usually do so because of a lack self-confidence. This is why self-confidence is a key element of achieving goals.

▷ **Misunderstanding of the Goal-Setting Process**

Many people mistakenly believe that goal setting is simply writing goals on paper, setting completion dates for them, and crossing them off when you achieve them. This mentality can hinder people from achieving success. Goals are not one-off tasks that you can simply cross off the list. They are the milestones of your life that guide you and show the world who you want to be or what you want to achieve.

▷ Inactivity and Lack of Commitment

Although many people have goals they want to achieve, few commit to them. And it's due to this lack of commitment that they often fail to go all out in order to achieve their goals. When it comes to goals (and to almost everything else in life) if you don't go all out, you will get mediocre results. This is why commitment is key.

Commitment alone is not enough, however. It needs to be combined with action. Without action, nothing will happen; there will be no progress. This is why a list of goals is useless on its own. It needs to be combined with actionable steps that outline what you need to do to actually get where you want to get.

Many people fall into the inaction trap when they reach a stage where they are satisfied with what they have and where they are in life. They stop chasing after bolder goals and sometimes even give up on goals they've had their whole lives. In short, they get stuck and stop trying to achieve extraordinary things.

Research tells us that the kind of satisfaction that leads to inactivity is either defined by enough happiness ("Why should I change anything? My life is ok as it is."), or not enough pain ("Why should I change anything? Things aren't so bad.") Indeed, happiness and pain are the only two factors that can cause people to take action and change their life in some way. This, however, does not mean that those who set goals and act on them necessarily start off feeling unhappy; it means they won't settle for "ok" or "not so bad."

What separates those who achieve their goals from those who don't is their commitment to keep taking action until they have reached their destination. So write down your goals, plan what actions you need to take to reach them, and commit to carrying them out, no matter what. This will help get you where you want to be.

▷ Analysis Paralysis

Analysis paralysis is a little bit like overthinking. It causes you to get stuck instead of moving forwards. Many people let their questions and doubts paralyze them. They believe that they cannot start setting goals unless they have answers to every "what-if" scenario. However, no matter how long you prepare and how hard you work, you will never get every-thing covered. You cannot foresee everything! In fact, even if endlessly analyzing seems like you're working towards your goal, it's actually the opposite: it keeps you from doing the work that will actually get you there. So what if you fail to foresee a hurdle along the way? So, what if you make a mistake? As you now know, progress involves endless adjustments and mistakes are amazing opportunities for growth. As Former US President Harry S. Truman wisely put it, "Imperfect action is better than perfect inaction." So don't try to figure everything out beforehand; start moving towards your goal, and you will find your answers in the process.

▷ Unclear Destination

People often set goals without having a clear vision of who they want to be or what they ultimately want to achieve. However, if you don't have a clear destination in your mind, it's hard to figure out what you need to do in order to get there. Your goals need to be clear; you need to be able to perfectly picture them in your head and be able to describe them to others. If you don't clearly understand the life you want, you run the risk of forever changing course and never realizing your full potential.

▷ Too Many Goals

Some people fall into the trap of setting too many goals for themselves. Doing so is like standing in front of a dartboard with one dart but wanting to hit three targets. It is challenging enough hitting one; it is impossible to hit three at the same time. Therefore, always aim to identify one main target to focus on and move towards. If this is a long-term goal that involves many steps, that's ok. Just break it down into smaller goals based on the steps you need to take and focus on those, one step at a time. Having too many big goals and things to achieve all at once can be overwhelming and cause you to quit before you even start.

Let's say you want to become a professional tennis player, for example. Where do you start? What are the steps to get there? As you are maybe lacking knowledge and experience, you may not know what steps are involved in reaching your final destination–and that's ok. In that case, your first step, or first small goal, would probably be to find someone who knows the steps involved, like a coach at school, for example. When you know what steps you need to take to reach your final destination, you can then concentrate your energy, time, and effort to get there.

To maximize your chances of success, see if you can eliminate all other secondary goals. You need to realize that you only have so much time and energy. So, choose goals that will bring you the highest ROE (return on effort) and focus on them.

HOW TO SET GOALS EFFECTIVELY

The process of goal setting forces you to think about the journey rather than just the final destination. Think of it like planning a holiday: to make sure that everything goes smoothly, you need to plan ahead. You need to choose your destination and research flights, hotel prices, the weather, and visa requirements. You need to decide how much time you want to spend on holiday and what you want to experience while you're there. Finally, you need to book everything and get to the airport.

As you can see, getting to your destination is not as simple as just deciding to go–and that's true with both traveling and going after your goals. Once you have a dream, you need a plan to achieve it. But remember: don't overthink it only to become trapped in an 'analysis paralysis' situation. You cannot be prepared for everything and there are bound to be some surprises along the way. So make a plan and accept that you might have to make adjustments along the way.

Let's say you want to go to college to study computer science. That would be your long-term goal–your destination. In order to get there, you need a plan that consists of smaller, short-term goals. For example, you need to have good grades at school to apply for college. You need to check college entry requirements. Would you need to pick up a programming language? Maybe you also want to gain work experience before attending college. An internship is an excellent way to do that...

This is just a simple example of how to begin forming a plan by breaking up a big long-term goal into smaller short-term goals. Let's now see how you can make sure that the goals you set–big or small–are set in a way that makes it easier for you to achieve them

1. Think About Your Desired Result

Your desired result must motivate you enough that you are willing to invest time in pursuing a goal. If it doesn't, then it's not worth pursuing. Your desired result must also be clear enough to you so that you can stay focused and avoid being distracted by irrelevant secondary goals that take you off-track. As you now know, having a good understanding of where you want to go is the best way to ensure you won't get lost on the way.

2. Create SMART Goals

Once you decide what you want, the next step is to set SMART goals. SMART goals are goals that are:

- **Specific**
- **Measurable**
- **Achievable**
- **Relevant**
- **Time-bound**

Specific goals are well-defined, precise goals. "I want to lose weight" is not specific. "I want to lose 25 pounds" is. Similarly, "I want to go to college" is not specific. "I want to study computer science at the University of Arizona" is.

Measurable goals are goals that are set in a way that makes it easier for you to stay on track and measure your progress. This usually means that for a goal to be measurable it should have a number attached to it. For example, you saying that you will study for next week's biology exam is not measurable. But if you say that you will study biology every day for 4 hours until next week's exam, then that is measurable.

Achievable goals are those that can be realistically achieved. For example, if you said that your goal was to lose 25 pounds in two weeks, that would not be achievable. By aiming to stick to such an impossible goal, you will end up feeling needlessly demoralized by a failure that you could not have done anything to prevent. This goal could not have been achieved no matter what you did. If, however, you said that you would lose 3 lbs in two weeks, then that's an achievable goal that you can work on and stay motivated along the way.

Relevant goals are those which are in line with what you want to achieve. For example, if you know that you need to work on your math in order to study computer science after you graduate, studying math for 2 extra hours a day is a relevant goal. On the contrary, deciding to lean how to swim is not. Even though it's not a bad goal to have, it's irrelevant to your current situations and plans and will less likely distract you from your ultimate goal, which is to study computer science. Ask yourself: "Do I need to learn to swim now? Do I have enough time? Will I be able to commit an extra 30 minutes 2-3 times a week?" When creating new goals for yourself, remember that there is no point in setting a goal just for the sake of setting it. Your goals should be milestones towards your chosen long-term destination.

Time-bound goals are goals that are linked to a realistic timeframe: a date when you want (and can realistically expect) to have met your goal. When it comes to goals that refer to some ongoing practice with no clear deadline, like studying math for 2 extra hours per day, then instead of a deadline you can set interim dates for when to review your goal. You might realize that 1.5 hours is actually enough for you to make progress, for example. How do you adjust your goal? Do you add extra material to study, or do you use these spare 30 min to do something creative?

So, let's now look at a few more examples of SMART goals.

Let's say you want to improve your endurance and start running. An excellent example of using the SMART technique would be: 'In three months from today, I want to be able to run 2 miles in under 30 minutes. In order to achieve this, I will run four times a week for 40 minutes.

Another example: 'From now on, I want to keep my room tidy. In order to achieve this, I will take 15 minutes every morning to make my bed, put my clothes away, tidy my desk and take any dirty dishes to the kitchen.

And the third one: 'In three months, I want to have saved $300 to spend on my outfit for the prom. In order to do this, I need to save $10 of my pocket money each week and work an extra 2 hours 5 times a week at the grocery shop.

3. Document Your Goals

When you document your goals, they become real and tangible, rather than vague ideas that only exist in your mind. Once you have your goals written out, put them in a prominent place–like your mirror or near your computer screen.

Doing that will serve as a daily reminder and motivation for what you've set out to achieve.

4. Create a Course of Action

Don't be afraid to be creative. Remember your creative and critical thinking skills and use them to develop the right course of action. For example, use crayons, markers, or colored pencils to write down your goals. Developing an action plan in this way activates different parts of your brain and strengthens your goals.

5. Create a timeline

As part of the action plan, create a timeline to help visualize the tasks, milestones, and deadlines for achieving goals. If your goal is shared with others, make sure to assign roles and responsibilities so everyone knows what they have to do. Once you plan everything out, try to comply with the timeline you have created as much as possible. A timeline creates a sense of urgency, motivating you to accomplish your goals as planned.

6. Take Action

Now that you have everything planned and documented, it's time to take action. You didn't go through all the previous processes to forget your goals. Every step you make should lead to another until you complete your goal.

7. Reassess and Evaluate Your Progress

You need to maintain a solid motivation to accomplish your goals. Consider scheduling a weekly assessment. Your assessment should include measuring your progress and checking your timeline to see how close you are to smashing your goal. Doing that will also help you stay motivated for the course. If you are a bit behind schedule, make the necessary adjustments and move on. This will allow you to succeed faster and more efficiently. It can inspire your ambitions and help you achieve tangible results.

SHORT-TERM AND LONG-TERM GOALS

We can divide goals into short-term and long-term goals. Short-term plans are those you intend to achieve within a short period–say in the next one week, one month, six months, or even one year. However, long-term goals cover a much larger period–for example, if you aim to become an aeronautics engineer when you grow up, you're making a plan for the relatively distant future.

However, it is worth noting that what qualifies as a long-term or short-term goal is quite relative. Also, your long-term goals can be made up of a series of short-term goals. Splitting your long-term goals into short-term goals will make them more easily attainable. You can also have mid-term goals that fall between your long-term and short-term goals.

Long-term goals might be something like graduating from college and everything you want to happen afterwards. Usually, your long-term goals determine your mid-term goals, and your short-term goals become steps toward achieving these larger goals. Looking at your goals in this format will help you realize that even the little things you do every day are vital for reaching the more important mid-term and long-term goals. Common long-term goals for teenagers include earning a bachelor's degree, starting a company, getting into your preferred career, etc.

. Mid-term goals relate to the plans for this academic year or your time at university, or the objectives you're planning to achieve in the next six months to two years. Mid-term goals are usually stepping stones to your long-term goals. However, they can also be independent goals. For example, you might have a goal of getting into a university, which is a mid-term goal that can bring you closer to your long-term goal to earn a bachelor's degree.

Short-term goals focus on the present. As mentioned, short-term goals are expected to be completed in a short time, like getting an A in an upcoming exam. But there is no set time-frame for such goals. It all depends on your overall timeline. For example, days can be used to measure the short-term goals of a one-month project. If you have a longer project with an overall timeframe of, say, one year, then short-term goals might have a one-month timeframe. Usually, people define short-term goals based on the timeframe of their mid-term and long-term goals.

TIPS FOR SMASHING YOUR SET GOAL

Like we said earlier, what is a goal if you can't achieve it? In order to set SMART goals, you can smash, you don't just need to write them down. You need to be smart about the way you approach them. So let's look at how you can set SMART goals in a way that maximizes your chances of success.

▷ Clarify Goals in a Positive Tone

When setting goals, try to avoid negatively stating your wishes. Instead of saying "I don't want to complain much," say, "Every day, I will note three positive things about my day in my diary before I sleep."

▷ Focus On the Process, Not the Result

This is one of the most challenging aspects of achieving your goals. Most times, you might focus too much on your goal while neglecting the process. But the most important thing to focus on is the process: the steps that will get you where you want to go. For example, suppose the result you want is to lose 20 lbs. This is your goal. But you shouldn't just focus on the number 20. While you're in the process of getting there, take time to notice when you have lost 5, 10, or 15 lbs. These milestones are equally important. Your goal was to achieve weight loss, and you're doing just that! Your success so far means that you are taking the right steps. Paying attention to the process might also help you re-adjust your goal as needed. For example, it might help you realize that your initial goal of losing 20 lbs is not right for your body, and that you should actually aim to shed 10 lbs instead.

▷ **Sign an Agreement with Yourself**

Once you are ready, whether in the preparation phase or the action phase, I recommend signing a contract with yourself to achieve success. That is almost like writing down your goals, but it is more formal and binding.

▷ **Visualize What You Want**

Imagination and mental exercise stimulate many neural networks that connect the brain's intentions to the body. So, take time to visualize your thoughts before setting and acting on your goals. This will help you to see the end result and will motivate you to move towards it.

▷ Embrace Support

Being supported from your loved ones can help you be more accountable and maximize your chances of success. Tell some friends or family members of your plan so they can encourage you and provide feedback when needed. Parents, teachers, or other adults you trust can provide you with valuable insights that could speed the process up or make it easier.

▷ Keep Your Goals Visible

As previously mentioned, it's very useful to put your goals, steps, and deadlines where you see them often. This will keep you motivated and help you work towards your goals more consistently.

▷ Reward Yourself

We all love to get rewarded for things we've achieved. Getting rewarded helps us realize that what we're doing matters and it keeps us focused on doing even more. Therefore, you can use this to fuel your determination and dedication to your goals. When you take a step towards your goal, be sure to reward yourself in the process. Rewards should be simple, consistent, easy to obtain, and healthy. For example, you may reward yourself by traveling long distances with your dog at the end of a hard day's work or after you have performed specific steps in your plan.

GOAL SETTING, IN A NUTSHELL

Here are the most important things you need to remember when it comes to setting goals. First and foremost, make sure you set goals that you really want to achieve. If you have a strong sense of purpose, you are less likely to give up when you encounter obstacles. If you do something just because your parents or other people want you to do it, this is not your goal, and you may find it harder to achieve it than if it was a personal decision.

Writing down your goals can help you organize your ideas and clarify your goals. Make sure your goals meet the SMART criteria. When you write down your goals, focus on what you will do instead of what you will not do. For example, if you aim to improve your health, set a goal of increasing your daily water intake. That will make you think more about water! However, if you focus on not drinking soda, you are likely to think about soda all day and end up consuming more.

After writing down your goals, place them in a prominent place to remind yourself of what you're aiming for. Looking at them every day will help you stay on track.

Finally, consider sharing your goals with friends, family, or classmates. Sharing your goals with people who care about you will help you feel supported and be accountable. Give everyone an opportunity to encourage you and cheer you on as you work towards your goals. In return, provide the same support for others' goals and dreams.

4

MONEY MANAGEMENT – BUDGETING, SAVING, AND SPENDING

Money drives the economy and everything therein. Even as a teenager, many aspects of your life depend on your money management skills. So don't delay working on these important skills just because you think they are only relevant to grownups. They are not.

We live in a world where spending is encouraged every-where-on Instagram, TV, blogs, etc. Everywhere you turn, there's a motivation to spend. Everyone will tell you what to buy, but no one teaches you how to earn or save money; it's not even taught at school. Therefore, you must take it upon yourself to develop these skills, apply them, and create the financial future you desire.

MONEY MAKING IDEAS FOR TEENAGERS

There are many and different ways you can earn money as a teenager. Whether you are an online person or more of a physical worker, there's something for you. So let's explore some money-making ways.

▷ Stream on Twitch

Believe it or not, many people make a living by playing video games and streaming their gameplay on Twitch. For example, Twitch streamer Jeremy 'DisguisedToast' Wang makes about $20,000 per month, depending on his viewership and the games he's playing. But bear in mind that not everyone makes that kind of money.

To get started, you'll need to be good at playing video games that people want to watch other people play (think Fortnite, for instance). You'll need a webcam and a computer capable of playing demanding video games or a current-gen system like the Xbox One. From there, you sign up for a Twitch account and begin playing video games. How many people subscribe to your channel to watch you play will determine how much money you make.

I just want to reiterate that things like that are possible, but it doesn't mean that if you decide to quit school tomorrow and become a professional online player, this will work for you. Remember that whatever decisions you make, you need to think them through.

▷ Gaming Competitions

If you're a competitive gamer, you can earn a decent income with gaming competitions. Of course, it won't be a full-time salary for most people, but if you win gaming tournaments for games like Fortnite, for instance, you can earn money. There are plenty of people who are examples of this. For instance, Bizzle–a competitive teenage gamer, makes over $300,000 playing in Fortnite gaming competitions. So, if you're good at some of these competitive games, you can probably make the most money playing in competitions (versus just streaming your gameplay on Twitch). But, again, remember, if you're already playing games in your free time, then it's worth giving a thought. You're enjoying your hobby and are also getting paid. However, if you're not really into games, don't set yourself a goal to become an online gamer just because the reward is tempting. I've already mentioned that building any skill takes time and experience. I'm sure that gamers who participate in these competitions have been playing for months if not years. But of course, if you think that you have what it takes or want to try it–go for it. The more things you try and learn, the more experiences you will have–and this will help you with building your critical and creative thinking skills.

▷ Start a Blog

The first thing you have to know is that blogging isn't a get-rich-quick scheme. It takes time and discipline to make actual money from it. In fact, it might take you over a year to even start making any money. For some it might happen quicker, of course, as there are exceptions. But in most cases, you should plan on writing at least every week for a year before you begin to build an audience and make money. So, if you have a passion for it, then better start now. A year from now, your blog might be taking off and earning you money!

To start a blog, you'll need a domain name and access to a hosting service–at a bare minimum. You can look for a domain name on sites like Namecheap and other domain name service providers, and you can find hosting through sites like Wordpress, Bluehost, or SiteGround, among others. Then, once your site is up and running, you can start blogging and building an audience.

The most regular ways to make money on blogs are through advertisements (think Google Ads) and affiliate marketing– which is when you link out to another product and get a commission if someone buys it (think Amazon).

You can also make money through memberships, creating products (like a course), offering consulting services, or having sponsored posts on your site (when a person or company pays you to write on your blog, usually to drive business to their company). Either way, it's a long journey, but if you stick to it, you can make some real cash from blogging.

▷ Become a Virtual Assistant

The Fair Labor Standards Act (FLSA) has made teenage online jobs harder to come by. It says workers must be at least 14 years old to have a non-agricultural job, and they must work limited hours. That figure jumps to 18-year-olds if the occupation involves hazards.

You can still find jobs for teens online, even if they're not posted on traditional employment search engines, like Indeed or LinkedIn. For example, being a virtual assistant provides a reliable way to earn money as a teenager. The position entails handling administrative tasks for someone while working remotely. Some of those responsibilities include:

- Email management
- Social media management
- Research
- Writing and editing
- Clerical tasks
- Basic bookkeeping
- SEO optimization
- Calendar organization

One way to find a virtual assistant position is through your social network. Perhaps your parents or friends know a business owner who needs help with day-to-day tasks. Bear in mind that the specific job description will vary between clients. Regardless, being a virtual assistant provides a great way to start earning money fast. Also, it gives you a window into how the corporate world works. It allows you to learn new skills like communication skills and several administrative skills including emails, booking appointments, arranging traveling, etc. This is a great way to understand the insides of the industry. Of course, this depends on what niche your client is and your VA responsibilities.

▷ **Online Tutoring**

Did you know that you can use your excellent grades in high school to make money? Thanks to tutoring platforms, you can turn your knowledge into a paycheck. Tutoring comes with flexible hours and the ability to set your pay rate.

You can sign up for sites like TutorCare (if you're at least 13 years old). TutorCare gives you oversight over your pay and hours and charges a commission rate of $12 per tutoring session. It even comes with free professional training if you want to improve as a teacher. You never know; you might find your future career as a teacher. Or it may help you see that perhaps teaching is not the full-time job for you.

▷ **Sell Stock Photos**

Opportunities to earn money licensing photos through stock sites are out there if you know your way around a camera. When you upload your content to Shutterstock, for example, the company pays you a 40% commission every time someone downloads your image. Of course, the exact paycheck depends on the retail price and how many people use your pictures.

The more photos you sell, the more Shutterstock pays. In addition, you can earn a pay bump when you hit certain uploading and selling milestones. Many other stock libraries, such as Alamy, Photoshelter, and Getty Images, have similar models.

▷ **Babysit**

Babysitting provides an option for many teens to earn extra money. The job comes with specific responsibilities and a reliable paycheck, making it one of the better-known ways to make money as a teenager.

If you've never babysat before, take a course from your local YMCA or Red Cross. You can also join babysitting websites, such as Care.com and Zum, to increase your chances of finding parents in need.

Parents frequently need help watching their kids, whether they're going out for the night or dealing with an emergency. According to a study from UrbanSitter, the average babysitter earns $16.75 per hour when they watch one child. Rates may vary depending on your location. Illinois has the highest minimum age requirement for babysitters at 14 years old.

▷ Mow Lawns or Remove Snow

If you're willing to get your hands dirty, start a lawn mowing business. People need lawn-mowing services from spring to fall, so there's always demand, especially among professionals, the elderly, and others who don't care to do physical labor.

This is a business that made R.J Duarte a lot of money. At age 8, he started cutting grass for people. Gradually, he turned the business into a company called Greenworx. Today, Greenworx makes millions of dollars for Duarte and his staff members.

You can expand your offering to include pulling weeds, raking leaves, watering plants, and painting fences. The more services you can provide someone, the more likely it is that they will become repeat customers.

Finally, if you live in an area with a snowy winter season, you can make money by shoveling or blowing snow and de-icing walkways.

▷ Dog Walking

Many people choose dog walking to make extra money, get some exercise, and hang out with dogs. They're great to hang out with! So this sounds like a win-win situation. You are getting the steps in and relaxing with a four-legged companion. If you already know someone else with a dog, try making them your first client. You can even set up a daily, weekly, or monthly schedule to plan your dog walks in advance.

You can also register with one of the many dog walking sites. These platforms let you create a profile where local pet owners can request your services. According to Indeed.com, the average dog walker makes $15.75 per hour.

▷ **Recycle**

You can make a few hundred dollars in cash collecting and recycling cans every month. Some states pay $0.05 – $0.10 for lightly used cans as a way to incentivize recycling. 11 states have container deposit laws, including:

- California
- Connecticut
- Delaware
- Hawaii
- Iowa
- Maine
- Massachusetts
- Michigan
- New York
- Oregon
- Vermont

▷ Clean Houses

If you like things in order, you might excel at cleaning other people's homes. You can start as a solo cleaner or work with a friend to tackle cleaning projects. Data from ZipRecruiter shows that house cleaners get paid $14 per hour on average.

House cleaning comes in two varieties: surface-level cleaning and deep cleans. Surface-level jobs target visible mess and untidiness. Cleaners at this level may offer dusting, vacuuming, mopping, and sweeping services. Deep cleaning takes more time and effort because it addresses hard-to-remove dirt and grime, which means it also pays more.

▷ Food Delivery

You can also earn extra cash for delivering food. For example, Instacart is an app that provides its customers with same-day delivery on groceries from their local store. The user does all of their shopping directly through the app and checks out. Once that's complete, the order is sent to a personal shopper (this is where you come in) to do the shopping and deliver the order that same day.

What's cool about Instacart, though, is that they offer both a full-service and in-store-only option. A full-service shopper goes to the designated store, does the shopping, packs it up, and delivers it directly to the customer (you leave the food on their doorstep in nearly all cases).

If that is too much, you can also be an in-store shopper, where you do the shopping and get the order ready for the customer to pick up. The in-store option is excellent for people who don't want to bounce around from store to store all day or make deliveries.

▷ Golf Caddy

If you live near an upscale golf course, you can apply as a golf caddy for a summer season. According to The New York Times, caddies can earn more than $100 for 18 holes. It's not too bad, considering that your primary responsibility is holding clubs for someone.

A golf caddy is important to a golfer's success. They serve as a confidant and an advisor for club selection. If you're good at your job, you can be the difference between an excellent round and a mediocre one. The same goes for the size of your post-round tip.

▷ Lifeguard

You need to know how to swim and be at least 15, but if you check both boxes, you are eligible to be a lifeguard. All lifeguards must take a course before they start earning a paycheck. The certification process ensures that the hire is a strong swimmer who understands how to administer first aid.

While you can garner a steady paycheck as well as a tan, make sure you're up for the responsibilities. Lifeguards have to handle emergencies that can be matters of life or death. If you don't want the pressure of donning the whistle and rescue tube, consider the other options on the list.

▷ Retail Worker

Many teens in the US make extra money working in retail. It is one of the most popular ways to make money. The position can be flexible and rewarding, especially if the company you choose has values that align with your own. For instance, if you're an aspiring fashion designer, apply for a job with a clothing store. Many retail stores pay minimum wage or close to it and hire people starting at age 16. The average hourly salary for retail workers is $14.12, with many high school students choosing the job to make some money on the side.

▷ Fast-Food Server

Next to retail, the fast-food industry is one of the largest employers of teenagers. While you probably don't want to work in fast food your entire life, it can be a great way to earn your first paycheck. Restaurants have a lot of open positions and hire people without industry experience.

Fast food experience can bolster your resume in several ways. First, working in a fast-paced environment teaches people how to adapt on the fly and meet tight deadlines. You may even parlay the job into working in a gourmet restaurant one day.

▷ Golf Course Worker

Making money as a golf course worker may appeal to you if you're not a social butterfly. You work with a small group of groundskeepers who ensure that a course remains in top shape. Don't worry; you don't need to know anything about playing golf to work there. Golf courses see an uptick in golfers during the summer, so clubs hire in late spring and early summer. Some core responsibilities include cutting grass, refilling water tanks, raking bunkers, and moving pins.

▷ Car Wash Attendant

If you have a passion for cars, get paid to clean them in your free time. Car wash attendants are responsible for taking orders, wiping the frame, and cleaning the glass. It's a simple way to make money as a teenager, whether you work for a local car wash or start a one-person crew.

If you decide to take the entrepreneurial route, ask your friends and family if they need a wash. Once you help everyone you know, start knocking on doors in your neighborhood and offering your services.

▷ Grocery Store Worker

The COVID-19 pandemic has forced people to reassess how "essential" their jobs are. Grocery store workers are among the few jobs that remain in demand, even in the face of a recession. Whether you work stocking groceries or slicing meats at the deli, there's always a way to make money as a teenager at a grocery store.

Many stores, including Kroger, Safeway, and Publix, hire kids as young as 14. As a result, you have a good chance of landing a position, even if you don't have previous experience. You'll likely start with entry-level tasks, like bagging groceries and collecting shopping carts, before graduating to more responsibility, like being a butcher or cashier.

▷ **Mystery Shopper**

Companies want unbiased feedback to figure out what they're doing well and where they can make improvements. So some places hire mystery shoppers to review their customer service, inventory, and cleanliness. It's free to sign up, as companies pay you to eat and shop at your favorite restaurants and stores. Mystery shoppers play a vital role in their local communities. They help make upgrades so that future shoppers can enjoy a better customer experience.

▷ **Movie Theater Attendant**

If you're a movie buff, apply to a movie theater. Attendants have a hand in keeping a theater operational year-round. That includes handling tickets, serving food and beverages, running the movies, and cleaning up after the shows. Movie theater jobs can provide valuable insight into the film industry if you aspire to make films. You'll also work with people your age and get free movie passes as a perk. The average attendant can expect to earn as much as $16.84 per hour.

▷ Barista

Baristas learn valuable customer service skills while working in a team-oriented environment. They can even flex their creativity when adorning coffee cups with frothy milk. Making a fantastic latte can be an art form!

Starbucks employs the most baristas globally, with more than 200,000 employees. You have to be at least 16 to apply for a job–unless you live in Montana, where the minimum age is 14. The average barista will make $10.57 per hour.

▷ Monetize Your YouTube Channel

If you have a YouTube channel with followers, you can use it to make money. YouTube allows you to run ads on your channel when you have at least 1,000 subscribers and 4,000 hours of watch time. If you want to earn money, kid-friendly content is a must.

The current algorithm favors creators that make longer videos because it gives YouTube more time to run ads. Length shouldn't come at the cost of quality, though. If you make a long video, maintain your production quality to attract new users.

▷ Manage People's Social Media Accounts

Teens have a leg up on adults in understanding social media. A 16-year-old grows up with apps like TikTok, Twitter, Instagram, and Facebook. Older people who were introduced to this technology later in life find it much harder to understand and use. Which explains why you can make good money fast by handling people's social media accounts.

Offering to tweet or post family members' content for a fee is a small-scale version of an advertising agency. Working as a one-person agency provides a glimpse into the advertising world while making money around the house.

These ideas can help you to make money as a teenager. However, with money-making comes money-spending. It is much easier for us to spend money than to make it. Therefore, you need to pay extra attention to how you spend your money. To that end, let's look at some tips that will help you spend wisely.

5 TIPS FOR SPENDING MONEY WISELY

If you don't want your hard-earned money to disappear in a whiff, you need to learn to spend money wisely. Here are some money tips that will help you spend your money in the best possible way.

1. Make Plans

Creating a plan, as with anything in life, is a good starting point. First, write down all your sources of income, excluding any allowances or money you received from your parents. Then write down your expenses. This will give you some insight into what money you have coming in and out, enabling you to manage your cash flow responsibly. Having a budget app can help you manage your funds on the go. Some apps can help you manage your funds and determine where you spend the most money. You will learn more about planning your finances later on, when we talk about budgeting.

2. Set Your Spending Goals

According to financial educator and founder of The Wela Way program, Nancy Phillips, one way to organize spending is the Giving, Investing, Saving, Spending (GISS) method. It helps you develop self-control and prioritize essentials. It suggests you choose a meaningful cause to donate a small percentage of your money (like 10%); invest a percentage in something essential (like your college fund), save a percentage for a rainy day; and then use the remaining percentage to buy things you need.

By setting a clear spending goal you can avoid overspending. Once you have a stable income, you have to develop a good habit of saving first and spending later. You can use the GISS method as a guide for how much you need to save. Don't forget that bills and other expenses are also taken from your "spending" pot, so make sure you have enough money to cover those before you splurge on anything else.

3. Cash First!

Unlike credit cards, which are notoriously easy to use and can lead to overspending, cash is more difficult to give away. Having a certain amount of money with you when you go out can help you spend within your budget and reduce temptation.

4. Resist Impulse Buying

Having money can make you feel an urge to spend it on things that are not actually important nor move you towards your long-term goals. This is known as "impulse buying." It what makes you spend money on the latest designer shoes, or even on last-minute items at the checkout line at the store (that you wouldn't even have thought of buying until you saw them there).

If you don't have to spend money, then don't. Hang out with friends at home instead of going out, cook your meals instead of ordering out, and look for as many free activities as possible. Making the most of what you possess will change your perception of essentials.

5. Keep Track of Your Money

It is always helpful to keep track of your expenses to determine how much you spent. Keep as many receipts as possible in a safe place. This way, you can also use them as a reference if your purchase is defective. If an item you bought stops working, you can't return, exchange, or get a refund for it if you don't have a receipt to prove that you purchased it.

Another great way to keep track of your funds is to have a budget. This is a way to calculate your earnings and track expenditures and it makes it easier to manage your money. So, let's look at how you can start budgeting.

7 TIPS FOR BUDGETING

1. Understand Your Income

Making money in your teens is a great feeling, but you will quickly understand that the promises you get salary-wise are different from what you actually earn. When you get your salary, you need to know how much will be getting before and after taxes—also known as total and net income.

Once you have determined this, add up any sources of income that do not require tax deductions, such as tips, gifts, bonuses, or allowances. To be on the safe side, if these numbers change over time, add up your income over the past few months and divide by the number of months to determine your average income, and start planning from there.

2. Plan Your Expenses

This is the less exciting part of budgeting. Just like you tried to understand your income, you should account for any potential expenses you might incur in a month. Some of these expenses will differ over time, so see if you can create separate budgets for each month. One of the easiest ways to manage your spending is using an app. Many apps allow you to create a digital budget on your phone. In addition, using apps will make it easy for you to carry your budget around for easy reference when needed.

3. Spend Wisely

We've touched upon this before, but it's very important to be wise with your spending. You are in a stage in your life where you will meet new people, get an eye-opening social experience, and buy things you have always wanted for yourself. However, although it is a good feeling to spend your money on the things you dream of, it can have a devastating impact on your financial future if it is not adequately managed.

If you can get one, a credit cards is an easy solution that can help you pay for certain expenses when cash is insufficient–plus it looks fancy. But be aware that you still need to pay it off, and if your salary is not high, this can be a daunting task. My advice would be that if you don't have money to buy something now, then don't buy it. If you really need it then save for it and buy it when you have the money.

If you are given a credit card, leave it home if you do not think you are going to need it. Credit cards are used more for emergency purposes or major purchases, not for those designer shirts or dresses that you see through shop windows.

A better option is the prepaid debit card. It gives a perfect introduction to managing your money without the major risks of credit cards.

4. Save for What You Need

During your teenage years, you are actively preparing for adulthood. Therefore, you need to learn how to become more self-reliant and save your money towards getting what you might need in the future. Later on, we will explore some tips on how to save your money.

Establishing long-term savings goals will help you manage your expectations for the significant life goals you wish to pursue–whether that's to buy your first car with your own money, to start your own business, or any other goals you might have. Saving for these goals from your teenage years will make them more attainable.

5. Take advice

Look, you may have that young pride that makes you think you know everything and question what adults tell you. "What do they know?" It's true that they have their flaws–we all do. But they have gone through the highs and lows of financial management and can help guide you.

Your parents are an excellent first source of advice. They can advise you on making the most of any allowance or income you get, so you don't have to beg them for cash every time. And remember, parents always want to help you if you just let them.

6. Learn About Inflation

As mentioned earlier, costs will change over time. Because of inflation, something that cost $100 a few months ago may now cost $105. Inflation is the steady increase in the price of goods or services, and you must bear it in mind when you budget. The inflation calculator provided by the US Bureau of Labor Statistics can help you calculate the future cost of things that increase in value over time.

7. The Divide and Conquer Rule

I call this the "divide and conquer" rule because it involves dividing your finances into percentages and dedicating each part to a separate class of expenses. You can apply this rule if you are unsure how much money should be set aside for expenses and personal financial goals.

One way to do this is the 50/20/30 method: you spend 50% of your income on any fixed expenses, 20% on savings, and 30% on any form of leisure you wish to enjoy. Sticking to a fixed number allows you to use your money to develop discipline, so you don't hear your parents nagging about why you spend so much money. You can combine this with the GISS method we talked about previously.

5 TIPS FOR SAVING MONEY

1. Open a Savings Account

A savings account can help you separate a large sum of money from your normal account, so that you cannot spend it. Many savings accounts also have interest rates, which means you can increase your funds faster. Interest rates are very low at the moment, so you will not get rich overnight. But it will serve the primary purpose–to keep part of your money safe from spending.

The best way to manage your savings account is to fund it regularly and withdraw only when it's essential. Set up a monthly direct debit to transfer a predefined amount from your salary or your monthly allowance into your savings account.

Different types of savings accounts provide various benefits and restrictions, so be sure to check the terms and conditions carefully to ensure that your account suits your personal goals and savings habits. Again, you might not be very keen on it but asking your parents could help you. They've probably been doing this for years! There is nothing shameful about asking for help. Ask for their advice, put together what you have found out and what you already know, and make a decision (critical thinking skills applied).

2. Save for Specific Goals

Setting a specific goal to reward your savings efforts can be a huge motivation to stay on track. It may be a particular item you want to spend money on, such as a new car or even a holiday, or it may be the amount you want to reach before a particular date.

Ensure your goals are ambitious but realistic. If you are too strict with your saving and force yourself to miss out on fun activities with friends, you will quickly become discouraged.

Whatever your goal is, keep track of it and remember to write down your progress. You will find that this will encourage you to stick to your plan and help you achieve your goals faster.

Develop a road map that shows how long it will take to accomplish this goal at the current savings rate. Check once a month to confirm if you are still proceeding normally and make adjustments if needed.

3. Review Your Spending

Before you start saving, it is best to understand your current financial management methods. For example, do you tend to run out before the end of each month, or do you often have a surplus? List all the things you often spend money on—such as food, clothes, travel, car insurance, gas, and evening outings. Are there areas where you might be overspending? Can you cut back a bit so that more money can be used to achieve your savings goals? Think where you can save—maybe those takeaway coffees can be replaced with home-made coffee? Can you buy clothes in a different store on sale rather than full price?

4. Think Before You Buy

Can you buy clothes in a different store on sale rather than full price? Compare prices before you make a purchase and think about where you could perhaps compromise. Maybe you can still go to a movie without splashing extra money on your popcorn. These are just ideas. I'll let you be the judge of this, as you're the one looking at your bank statement or your spending list.

Study your bank statements for the past three months. Write down your expenses and savings and set some realistic goals for yourself. Try using an online budget tracker to help you understand where your funds are going.

Finally, and I know that I keep throwing parents into this (it can also be any other adult that you trust) but go and have a conversation with them about how they save. You wouldn't believe what tricks they can have up their sleeves. And they will be happy to share what they know with you.

5. Keep At It!

Saving money feels like a long way out, but it's essential to stick to it. If you encounter challenges along the way, don't be discouraged. Everything takes time and patience. Enjoy the process! As long as you keep your money aside and resist the temptation to spend your money frequently, you will achieve your ultimate savings goal. Be consistent, and don't forget to reward yourself. Then, once you've reached your target, set yourself another one!

Money management is essential for you as a teenager. From making money to spending it, you have to make proper decisions. Failure to plan your finances might result in a lack of funds or missed opportunities (where the opportunity involves monetary investments). Therefore, use the tips I've given you, develop your money management skills, and take your finances to a higher level.

5

TIME IS MONEY; MANAGE IT!

As a teenager, you have a lot of responsibilities–especially if you're determined to work on your life skills and smash your goals! So it's normal if you feel a bit overwhelmed at times. However, feeling overwhelmed is not a pleasant feeling. Luckily, you can avoid it if your practice a little thing called **time management**.

Time management is essential in every one of your endeavors. Whether you are a teenager or already entering adulthood, proper time management is a critical life skill that you must learn and apply to your daily life. Time management skills are essential because most of us don't use time efficiently. As Seneca, a stoic philosopher pointed out, it's not that we don't have enough time to achieve great things in our lives; we just end up wasting a lot of it.

Having time-management skills is about taking charge of your own time so that can do not only things that you have to do (like homework, extra curriculum hours, and home chores), but also allocate time to things that you want to do (like your hobbies, going to the movies, and meeting up with your friends).

Can you recall a time when you had to study for an extra hour, tidy up your room, but also wanted to spend an hour playing the guitar, reading a book, or doing something else, but could not find the time to do everything? Why do you think that was? Was it perhaps because you wasted time scrolling on Instagram, or browsing the web with no real aim? Or maybe it was simply because you added too many things on your to-do list and got overwhelmed.

If wasting time is usually the culprit for you, there is room for improvement. Mindlessly scrolling through social media and the web is what we call a "low-value" activity. The time you spend on such activities should be reduced if you want to get more valuable things done.

If you tend to add too many things on your list and get overwhelmed, then it's ok, you're not alone! That can be managed, too. Later on, we will go into more detail on how to avoid feeling overwhelmed and stressing yourself out.

Time management is defined as the efficient use of your time. Think of time management as a combination of efficient work and prioritization. People who are good at time management know how to approach their tasks in the best way possible; at the same time, they are good at figuring out what needs to be done in what order and know how to manage distractions. They understand the difference between urgent and important tasks.

Say, for example, that you have a test tomorrow, but you haven't studied yet. To study for your test would be an urgent task. Walking your dog when it hasn't been walked for long hours is also an example of an urgent task. Working on an assignment can also be considered an urgent task, if the deadline is fast-approaching. However, if your deadline is five days away, then it's likely that your assignment is an important task, but not an urgent one. Important tasks are critical and failing to do them may have severe consequences for you or others around you. But provided that you have allocated enough time to work on them later, you don't need to prioritize them over other, more urgent, tasks.

If you also have an excellent understanding of this, prioritizing the tasks on your to-do list will become much more manageable and you can make the best use of your daily 24 hours. It's important to understand that all successful people understand the importance of time and time management–and they're very good at it!

THE IMPORTANCE OF TIME MANAGEMENT

Let's now look at why time management is so important and why you should care to develop strong time-management skills even in your teenage years.

▷ **It Improves Performance**

Scheduling your essential tasks will help you better understand everything you need to do and how long each task will take. When you have a timeline to follow, you will find that you waste less time deciding what to do, eradicate procrastination and give yourself more time to focus on your tasks. Building this skill is not about having a rigid schedule and attending to tasks robotically with no joy. No, not at all! The point is to know yourself better and learn about your day, optimize it, and still have time to be spontaneous and have fun! Time management enables you to focus on the essential tasks before you and avoid time-consuming distractions such as texting, checking your emails every 10 minutes, and browsing the web.

▷ **It Helps You Deliver Quality Results**

One known reason for substandard delivery in whatever we do is inadequate time, which necessitates rushing through our tasks. When you rush to complete your task, you are prone to making avoidable–and sometimes costly–mistakes. Think about times when you had to submit your paper at school and had to rush through it because you left it too late!

You didn't have time to check it. Maybe you had great ideas but couldn't execute them as doing so would have meant missing the deadline.

It is always much better to start working on things earlier. When you don't have to rush to complete a task, you can put more energy and thought into it and get the best result possible. Time management can help you schedule and prioritize tasks to ensure you have enough time to complete them to the best of your ability.

▷ It Builds Your Confidence

When you manage your time correctly and complete tasks on time, you will feel a sense of accomplishment and confidence in your abilities. It's a great feeling when a task is complete and can be removed from your list. Consistently completing your tasks is a significant motivating factor that boosts your confidence and helps you achieve even more. It is a positive reinforcement that keeps you going.

Don't get discouraged if some of the tasks will not get done or take longer to accomplish than you thought. You will get better with time as you build experience, and you will be more precise with estimating time correctly. Always remember that consistency is key.

▷ It Increases Efficiency

When you learn how to manage your time efficiently, it helps you stay more focused on whatever you are doing.

That, in turn, allows you to accomplish more in a shorter period of time. For example, suppose you have a significant task (like helping your mum plan your sibling's birthday party) and another minute task (like tidying up your room). Planning a birthday party takes more than 15 minutes and doing it before school is not the best idea. Being efficient and not wasting these 15 that you have to spare before school–you can tidy up your room instead. You would then be able to cross one job off your list. So now, after school, you can concentrate on helping your mum organize your sibling's party–and any other tasks from your list.

Time management will help increase your efficiency in planning your tasks to fit perfectly with your time. And, as I've said earlier, you should develop this skill regardless of your age. Like every other skill we've explored so far, everyone can gain time-management skills if they put their mind to it.

Time management makes life easier for you. It might be difficult if you have never done it before, but it will be great once you get the hang of it. It will give you pride of accomplishment and will boost your confidence. So let's explore some techniques that will help you develop those much-needed time-management skills.

TIME-MANAGEMENT TECHNIQUES

You'll often hear people talking about how they manage their time. You must know that time management can be rather subjective; what works for someone else might not work for you. You have to take it upon yourself to develop a time-management method that suits you. That said, there is a blueprint that can help you make proper decisions on dividing your time among tasks. Let's take a look.

Audit Your Time

The first step to developing time-management skills and creating an effective schedule is to do a time audit. By this, I mean that you should take a look at each of your tasks and determine how long it takes you to complete them. Make a list of everything you do in a day, starting from getting out to going to bed. How long it takes to get ready in the morning, have breakfast, etc? Write it all down. Walking or riding to school, time at school, and after-school activities. What do you do when you come back home? Add everything to your list. How long you do your homework for, how long you spend on your hobbies, chores, after-school/college classes, scrolling on social media, texting–and everything else. Keep doing it for a week; what you do and how long it takes you. After a week, you will have a better picture of how you spend your time. At the beginning of the book, there is a link where you can sign up to get a free spreadsheet to help you track your daily activities, along with goal-setting templates, and much more.

Since we can't, unfortunately, have more than 24 hours a day, you need to manage how you use them as efficiently as possible. When you review your time, you reverse-engineer your daily behavior to determine which areas you are efficient and productive in, and which are not. After noting down your daily tasks and times, you will be able to spot where your time is spent well and where you're possibly wasting it. With this information, you can rearrange your daily schedule and manage your time before and after school more effectively.

Auditing your time requires some planning and discipline, because–I will not lie to you–this can be a tedious task. However, if you want to master time management, then the data you collect during the audit will be invaluable to help you create new routines, habits, and systems. In addition, these compiled data can improve your efficiency and help you make profound positive changes in your life. And if you're wondering what's the best way to go about doing your audit and timing your tasks, it's really quite simple.

First, set a 1-hour countdown timer every hour, or set an alarm clock to sound once every hour–whatever works for you. Then, take a few minutes at the end of each hour to record what you did during that hour. You can use a pen and notepad, Word, your Notes app, or a spreadsheet to do this.

Another way is to note the time whenever you are about to begin working on a task–and do that throughout the day. For example, "It is 05.15 pm, and I am checking my inbox." You will record another entry when you switch tasks or do anything unrelated to checking your inbox, so you'll be able to tell from your notes how long checking your inbox took you.

The first day you try this, you might forget to record what you are doing from time to time. If that happens and you only get part of the data for the day, repeat the process the next day until you get the data for the whole day. The length of time you choose to run the audit for is up to you. Of course, the more data you have, the more meaningful it will be. Therefore, I recommend that you do this time audit daily for at least a week. You can also do it randomly for a few days in a month. However, this might necessarily drag out the process and your audit will linger on your to-do list as an uncompleted task. So get it done, and then move on to your next task.

After collecting the data, you can then proceed to analyze your records. When going through these records, there will be some areas that you'll recognize immediately as areas that require improvement. Maybe you're the person who leaves a house in a rush every morning. That can be fixed if you so desire. You need to analyze why this is happening. Is it because you get up too late? Do you keep snoozing the alarm? Or maybe you're getting out of bed after the alarm rings but losing your valuable time when you're getting ready? That is for you to decide, and it could be that the problem you identify can be addressed with minimal adjustments. Perhaps setting the alarm clock 15 minutes earlier is all you need in order to enjoy rush-free mornings. However, there will also be those tasks that require you to put in a bit more work to address.

Once you have audited your time, you will understand how you can start reconstructing your activities in order to be more efficient with your time. So, to put it simply, going through this activity helps you take the guesswork out of time management.

Write a To-Do List

Time management involves planning out what to do with the time you have–and a to-do list helps you do just that. When it comes to managing your time, noting your action plan down in a physical or digital journal or activity manager can be a game-changer.

Having performed an audit, you now you possess valuable information about your daily schedule; you can see where and how much time you spend on your activities throughout the day.

Now you can start working on your to-do list. Start by brainstorming and writing down everything you need to do, from doing your homework to meeting up with your friends. Everything. You can start with the things you need to do and those you want to do. Your to-do list can focus on the following day, or even the whole week.

We all have plenty, and in some cases, hundreds of tasks that need to be completed sooner rather than later. These tasks can range from the incredibly boring to the fun and exciting. Here are some examples:

- Clean the fish tank
- Walk the dog
- Get the oil changed in the car
- Help mum to arrange a party for a sibling
- Set short-term personal goals
- Set short-term academic goals
- Look into gym options
- Check what after-school classes are available
- Learn to play an instrument
- Do laundry
- Meet with friends
- Play tennis
- Do homework
- Add an extra hour on Tuesdays to study science

If you're finding it hard to get the list going, then see if you can add even the simplest of tasks, like:

- Get out of bed
- Brush teeth
- Get dressed
- Have breakfast

Write all your tasks down on your phone, a piece of paper, or wherever you prefer. Don't over-analyze and overthink. Just note it down. Make sure to refer back to the information you collected during your audit to make sure you don't forget anything. Once you have your list, the fun can begin!

Start from small tasks on your list, crossing them out as you finish them. This will help you get into a habit of using your to-do list as a roadmap for your day. As time goes by, you will notice that these smaller tasks will probably stop making it into your list; you will get so used to doing them that they will naturally blend into your everyday life. Other tasks will replace them, and your to-do list will evolve. But take it one step at a time; we all have our own pace and no one's day or life is the same. The important thing is that you get into the habit of making a to-do list.

Prioritize Your To-Do List

1. The Musts/Wants/Bonuses Method

So, as you probably know, it's very hard to get anything done if you treat every task with the same urgency. This is why you need to learn to prioritize. All your tasks cannot be classified as urgent—this is sure to make you feel overwhelmed and stressed out. We've already talked about how some tasks—even though important—are not urgent. You need to look at your tasks and figure out which ones fall under each of these two categories. Let's now look at one way you can do this.

First, take a piece of paper (you can also do this digitally if you prefer) and divide your tasks into three columns: Musts (these are your urgent tasks), Wants (these are your important but not urgent tasks; you will only get to do them once your Musts are done), and Bonuses (these are fun tasks; you will only get to do them once your Musts and Wants are done).

Musts are tasks that MUST be done. You have no choice. This column shouldn't have more than three or four things, as you need to make sure that they're always done first. These things will most probably have to do with school or your job (if you have one). The idea is not to have a long list, as your Musts are tasks that you will probably have to repeat daily, in one form or the other. Don't overwhelm yourself; otherwise, you will panic, and nothing will get done.

Wants are tasks that also need to be done, but only after you've completed and crossed out all your Musts. These can be things like your hobbies, working out, or cooking. Let's say, for example, that you're learning to dance. You want to do this, but if you have an assignment coming up or you're not ready for an upcoming exam, you will have to say 'no' to your dance class–at least until you've finished with your schoolwork.

Bonuses are tasks that don't necessarily need to be done, but that you love doing. They can be things like going shopping, getting your hair done, playing a video game for as much as you want, or hanging out with friends. You should only get to them once you have completed your Musts and Wants. This way, you'll also get to enjoy them more, as you'll have peace of mind that you're not falling behind on any of your responsibilities. Plus, they are a great source of motivation to get everything done!

Once you have all your tasks divided into these three categories, you need to make sure that your tasks are actionable. The more specific you are with your tasks, the more likely it is that you will complete them. Let's look at two examples of to-do lists to help you understand the difference between actionable and non-actionable tasks.

List 1

- Groceries
- Cookies
- Dentist appointment

List 2

- Go to the grocery store to get cauliflower and aubergines
- Bake chocolate chip cookies
- Call my dentist and book an appointment for next Friday

The tasks on the first list serve more like reminders, while those on the second list are actionable tasks. They indicate exactly what you need to do. This is the way you should aim to frame your tasks: be specific–what steps do you need to take to accomplish your task? It is easier to accomplish a goal or task if it is clear because it encourages and motivates immediate actions and decisions. In contrast, a vague plan may require you to stop and consider how to go about completing it.

2. The Today/Tomorrow/7 Days/30 Days Method

There is another method to prioritize your to-do list, which involves dividing your tasks into four columns: Today (these are tasks that need to be completed within the next 24 hours), Tomorrow (these are tasks that need to be completed within the next 48 hours), 7 Days (these are tasks that need to be completed within one week), and 30 Days (these are tasks that need to be completed within one month).

If you're finding it challenging to decide which task should go where, think about what will happen if a task is not completed within either of those given timeframes. For example, let's say you have to submit a biology assignment in 7 days. What will happen if you put your task "to work 2 hours on my biology assignment" in the 7 Days column? Most likely, you will not submit your assignment on time. So this task has to go in the Today and possibly the Tomorrow column, too, depending on how much time you need to prepare your assignment.

3. The 1-3-5 Method

You could also use the 1-3-5 Method, which is when your list for the day contains one big important/urgent task, three tasks of medium importance, and five small tasks. That is particularly useful when you have an extensive list, as it forces you to identify the most important tasks. As always, make sure the most urgent and vital stuff goes at the top.

4. Schedule

Some tasks on your to-do list will take only a few minutes to complete—like taking the dirty dishes from your room to the kitchen. When it comes to such tasks, you can start by crossing them off first. Doing so is an easy way to start off your day feeling like you've already accomplished something—plus, it will allow you to concentrate on your other tasks.

When it comes to urgent or important tasks that you know will take you a long time to complete, make sure to schedule them in, carving out as much time as you need to complete them. You can then organize less important tasks on your to-do list around them (either before or after).

You can do the same with tasks that you know you have to do every day at the same time. Do you need to take out the dog every evening at 8 o'clock? Make sure to schedule it in, so that you know how much time you have left for your other tasks.

When writing your to-do list, always think about how completing tasks on it helps bring you closer to your goals. Remind yourself why each task is essential. This will help motivate you to complete the task. It is much easier to work with a purpose than aimlessly executing task after task.

A to-do list is an integral part of managing your time well, and you should schedule some time each day or at the beginning of each week for you to write down everything you have to do. You could do this as part of your morning routine or maybe before you go to bed as part of your evening routine. Studies show that spending five minutes writing a to-do list before bed could actually help you sleep better, as it helps get your to-dos out of your head and onto paper, quieting your mind and preparing you for sleep.

If you put what you've learned here into practice, combined with the other life skills we've covered, you can expect to have many productive and fulfilling years ahead of you–starting from today! Before I let you go, however, there's one more important thing we have to cover...

6

SOCIAL MEDIA

While developing the life skills you need to navigate your teenage years, you need to pay attention to social media. Social media has become an essential part of our lives in the 21st century. Therefore, it is worth putting in the effort to ensure that you use social media platforms to your advantage. Because, if you don't pay attention to how you use social media, you might find yourself at a disadvantage—and that may be costly for you and your future aspirations.

We are social creatures. We need the company of others to thrive in life, and the strength of our connections has a monumental impact on our mental health and well-being. Establishing social connections with others can relieve stress, anxiety, and depression. It can improve self-worth, provide comfort and happiness, prevent loneliness, and even extend life. Conversely, a lack of strong social connections can pose severe risks to your mental and emotional health.

Today, loads of us rely on social media platforms (such as TikTok, Facebook, Twitter, Snapchat, YouTube, and Instagram) to connect with others. Although each has its benefits, it is essential to remember that social media and the social networking they allow for can never replace real-world relationships. Face-to-face contact with others is required for the triggering of those hormones which help relieve stress and which make us feel happier, healthier, and more active. The irony is that for a technology designed to bring people closer together, social media can make you feel lonelier and exacerbate mental health problems, such as anxiety and depression.

So, let's begin by defining social media. When we think of the word "media," it usually reminds us of traditional media such as newspapers, magazines, and television. However, when you add the world "social" to the mix, the resulting term presents a unique notion. Social media adds technical components and flexibility to how people consume, share, and collaborate on the content presented. In short, social media can best be described as an internet-based way to publish or broadcast digital content readers can fully interact with.

Anyone can post on social media. Traditional news media like CNN and Fox News publish their content for digital consumption. The same is true for businesses and organizations. Every local football club can use social media to post content for members to read, watch and interact with.

Before continuing, I want to point out an interesting observation. Many people think of social media and social networking as being one and the same. However, they are different. As we've already established, social media refers to any and all platforms where content is published with an aim to get an audience to interact with it. Social networking, however, refers to the relationship between users of said social media.

Let's look at Facebook, for example. Facebook is a social medium, as it allows anyone (individuals, businesses, and organizations) to create a page where they can share content. At the same time, however, it allows you to connect with your friends (or any Facebook user for that matter). You can message each other and share content (including non-Facebook-based content). This is social networking. So Facebook is a social medium through which people network with one another.

Interestingly, the first platform for social networking was launched in 1977 and was called Sixdegrees.com. It allowed users to set up profile pages, create connection lists, and send messages within the network. The site accumulated approximately 1 million users before it was acquired for $125 million. It closed down in 2000, but it then made a mild comeback and is still in operation today.

A little more than 40 years since the launch of Sixdegrees.-com, we now find ourselves in a world dominated by social media. It's therefore worth taking a step back to consider how these platforms may be affecting us–both positively and negatively.

THE POSITIVE IMPACT OF SOCIAL MEDIA

+ Connecting With Others

Having a social network is very important and positively impacts mental health and well-being. Having one online allows you to connect with like-minded peers, regardless of how far away from you they are geographically. This is especially useful for those who don't feel like they have a good support network to turn to at their home, school, or local community.

+ Sharing Knowledge and Learning Opportunities

If you know which sources and content creators to turn to, social media platforms can be an amazing source of information about anything you can think of–academic or not. Importantly, social media can help young people access information that they may not be comfortable seeking offline, like information on mental health and well-being. And, crucially, they can help you share your knowledge with the world, too!

+ Reach Out or Offer support in Difficult Times

Social media allow people to reach out to a wide audience when they need help. For example, say you're trying to raise funds for a particular venture but cannot do it all yourself. You can leverage the interconnectivity and networking that social media offer to raise the money you need from people who are open to helping that specific cause. Similarly, social media allows you to see people or projects that you want to support.

+ Platforms for Creativity

Another benefit of social media is that they are a great source of inspiration, as they expose people to each others' creativity. People from all sorts of different backgrounds and cultures share their techniques, styles, and ideas, creating opportunities for never-before-seen diversity in our collective creativity.

THE NEGATIVE IMPACT OF SOCIAL MEDIA

– Poor Sleep, Eye Fatigue, and Lack of Exercise

Social media can be incredibly addictive. We all know what it feels like to tell ourselves that we will only check our notifications, only to end up scrolling mindlessly for hours without even realizing it. In addition, if you use your device before going to bed and you don't use a blue-light filter, then staring at the screen will have a harmful effect on your sleep.

Our brains confuse the screen's blue light with daylight and wake us up thinking that it's morning! We also blink much less when looking at a screen, which can cause eyestrain and fatigue. So when your parents ask you to leave phones and other gadgets in another room at night, now you know why.

— Feeling Like You're Not Good Enough

Even when you know that the pictures you see on social media are carefully curated and manipulated, they can still make you feel insecure about your appearance–and of your life as a whole. Even though some people share content that is more honest, most still promote the best version of themselves and only share the highlights of their lives; the harsh reality of their everyday lives is often hidden from public view. Still, that doesn't reduce the feelings of envy and dissatisfaction you have when scrolling through a friend's FaceTuned photos of their beach holiday, or when you are reading about their exciting academic achievements.

— Fear of Missing Out (FOMO)

Although FOMO has been around for much longer than social media, sites like Facebook and Instagram seem to exacerbate the feeling that other people are more interesting than you or live a better life than you. Thinking that you're missing out on something can affect your self-esteem, cause anxiety, and drive more social media use. FOMO may force you to pick up your phone every few minutes to check for updates or respond to every alert-even if it means you are wasting valuable time that you could be spending on working on your goals and actually creating the life of your dreams.

— Feelings of Loneliness and Isolation

Studies have shown that frequent use of social media cause younger people to experienced increased feelings of emotional loneliness. In fact, reducing your use of social media can make you feel less lonely, less isolated and improve your overall well-being. This is because the less time you spend on social media, the more you will interact with the people (actually) around you, which is much more beneficial when it comes to not feeling lonely or isolated.

— Depression and Anxiety

We all need physical contact with friends and family once in a while to maintain mental health. There is nothing faster or more effective to reduce stress and improve your mood than some face time with people who care about you. The more you prioritize social media connections over face-to-face relationships, the greater your risk of developing mood disorders such as anxiety and depression.

— Cyberbullying

Cyberbullying is a very sensitive issue and has the most significant negative impact on social media. Social media platforms like Twitter may become hotspots for spreading hurtful rumors, lies, and abuse, leaving lasting emotional scars.

— Misinformation and Disinformation

Social media allow anyone to share information, regardless of how true it is. This has led to two very serious problems: misinformation and disinformation. The difference between the two lies in the intention of the content creator. The term misinformation is used to describe content that is false, but which has not been created with an intent to trick anyone; it's by accident–not that that makes it any less dangerous to believe or share. Disinformation, on the other hand, is false information that has been created to manipulate and deceive–usually to promote a certain agenda. Being able to spot misinformation and disinformation is crucial. Some obvious red flags to keep an eye out include: headlines in all caps, spelling mistakes and typos, egregious claims, and lack of sources. In any case, always use your critical thinking skills when consuming content on social media; take the time to question whether what you're watching or reading is true.

— Scams and Hacking

Social media are ripe with scams. The best advice I can give you is that if something sounds too good to be true, it probably is. No one is giving away iPhones for free, you have not been randomly chosen for a free trip to Hawaii, and there is indeed a chance that your new secret admirer might be catfishing you. It's always best to take a moment before you agree to anything so that you can put your critical thinking skills to good use! Finally, don't forget to change your passwords frequently to avoid getting hacked–and never share any information that could be used to bypass any security questions on your accounts or lead to identity theft.

4 TIPS ON LOOKING AFTER YOUR MENTAL HEALTH

Your mental health is important, so let's see what you can do to make sure it's not negatively affected by social media.

1. Spend Less Time Online

Track how much time you spend on social media daily. Then set a goal for how much time you want to reduce and make a plan on how you're going to achieve that goal (like you learned in Chapter Three). For example, you can turn off your phone at specific times during the day, leave your phone in another room at night, disable social media notifications, or even delete some social media applications from your phone so that they're only accessible via your computer.

2. Consider Healthier Alternatives

If you're browsing social media because you are bored, go for a walk and do something creative instead. Feeling lonely? Invite friends out for coffee. Are you moody? Go for a run!

Even though social media are convenient quick fixes, there are usually healthier and more effective ways to satisfy your needs.

3. Express Gratitude

Feeling and expressing gratitude for essential things in life can ease the resentment, hostility, and dissatisfaction that social media sometimes generate. Reflect. Try to write a gratitude journal or use a gratitude app. Record all the good memories and positive aspects of your life and the things and people you feel grateful for. The more often you do this, the better.

4. Practice Mindfulness

Experiencing FOMO and comparing yourself disadvantageously to others will make you addicted to the disappointments and frustrations in life. Instead of focusing on the present, you focus on "what if." That will prevent you from living the life that truly befits you. By practicing mindfulness, you can learn to live more in the present, reduce the impact of FOMO, and improve your mental health.

3 WAYS TO STAY SAFE ONLINE

Let's now look at some tips for staying safe while using social media.

1. Check Your Privacy Settings

The best starting point is to check the privacy settings of any social media network you are using. The default privacy settings on most social media platforms will give your posts the most public exposure, which can be dangerous. It's always best to only share your posts with people you actually know.

2. Think Twice Before Posting!

Your social media security is directly related to the personal information you allow others to view. Limit your profile and don't include your personal information in posts. Never give out your phone number or address. Keep private information confidential. Don't post anything you wouldn't want your parents, teachers, college admins, or employers to see.

Content that's published on the internet is never permanently deleted and can... come back to haunt you.

3. Sometimes, Sharing Is NOT Caring

Sometimes you may be tempted to talk about sex on social media, or even share nude photos. Talking about sex with strangers can be very dangerous, as it can be a sign of grooming and predatory behavior, which can have horrible consequences. So, please, avoid it at all costs. Furthermore, you should never share nude photos (even with your boyfriend or girlfriend). Aside from the fact that they can be leaked, which would be a nightmare experience, they can also make you vulnerable to extortion and cyber bullying, as well as cause extremely serious legal issues. In some states, exchanging nude photos of minors is considered a felony–even if the images were taken and shared with mutual consent by the minors involved. Teenagers who receive photos may be charged with child pornography, even if they did not request a copy of the image. So, again, please avoid it at all costs.

Despite their disadvantages, social media can be a great addition to your life–provided that you use them carefully. Explore them to your benefit, use them as a source of inspiration, reach out to others, and make meaningful connections that will aid your goals in life. Apply the other life skills you've learned to help you make proper decisions online and offline, and see your teenage years become as blissful and fruitful as you desire.

CONCLUSION

Growth comes with new wonders, challenges, and responsibilities. Which is why you need to be well-prepared in order to make the most of this period in your life. If you think of life as a journey, you're really just getting started. In order to avoid getting lost along the way, you need a compass. This is exactly what the life skills we covered in this book are. They will help guide you and help you stay on track. They will help you make the right decisions in order to achieve your goals and confidently reach your destination in life–whatever that may be. They will help you be the best version of YOU!

If you enjoyed this book, please take a few moments to write a review of it.
Thank you!

A GIFT TO OUR READERS

The purchase of this book includes goal setting, time
management and budget worksheets.
Let's start working on it.
Please scan QR code
Or visit
Davidskiddy.com
To let us know where to deliver it to

RESOURCES

Here are some resources that you might find useful:

FACT CHECKERS

FactCheck.org

https://www.factcheck.org/

Politifact

https://www.politifact.com/

Snopes

https://www.snopes.com

YOUTUBE VIDEOS

Sprouts Schools, Creative Thinking: How to Increase the Dots to Connect

https://www.youtube.com/watch?v=cYhgIlTy4yY

Samantha Agoos (TED-Ed), 5 tips to improve your critical thinking

https://www.youtube.com/watch?v=dItUGF8GdTw

Valorian, 6 Steps To Increase Your Creativity Everyday

https://www.youtube.com/watch?v=Pth60EWA8Qs

Rachel Catherine, Time Management Tips

https://www.youtube.com/watch?v=CFiBtP_Fxuk&t=1s

BRAIN GAMES AND BRAIN TRAINING WEBSITES

Verywellmind.com

https://www.verywellmind.com/top-websites-and-games-for-brain-exercise-2224140

Sharpbrains.com

https://sharpbrains.com/blog/2008/05/26/brain-games-and-teasers-top-50/

REFERENCES

(c) Copyright skillsyouneed.com 2011-2021. (n.d.). *Critical thinking | SkillsYouNeed*. Skills You Need - Helping You Develop Life Skills. https://www.skillsyouneed.com/learn/critical-thinking.html

24 time management tools for teens. (2020, January 18). Choosing Your Battles. https://choosingyourbattles.com/time-management-tools-teens/

9 great brain training websites and games. (n.d.). Verywell Mind. https://www.verywellmind.com/top-websites-and-games-for-brain-exercise-2224140

Alban, P., & DC. (2021, August 11). *How to be more creative: 10 proven techniques*. Be Brain Fit. https://bebrainfit.com/be-more-creative/

A beginner's guide to goal setting for teens. (2021, January 25). Powerful Youth. https://powerfulyouth.com/beginners-guide-goal-setting-for-teens-smart-goals/

Chapter 7: Critical thinking and evaluating information | EDUC 1300: Effective learning strategies. (n.d.). Lumen Learning – Simple Book Production. https://courses.lumenlearning.com/austincc-learningframeworks/chapter/chapter-7-critical-thinking-and-evaluating-information/

Collections archive. (n.d.). Snopes.com. https://www.snopes.com/collections/

Creative thinking skills | College success. (n.d.). Lumen Learning – Simple Book Production. https://courses.lumenlearning.com/suny-collegesuccess-lumen1/chapter/creative-thinking-skills/

Creative thinking, creative solutions, creative change. (n.d.). Teenage Whisperer Troubled Teens Challenging Behaviour Youth at Risk Adolescent Mental Health – Troubled Teens Challenging Behavior, Challenging behaviour. https://www.teenagewhisperer.co.uk/creative-thinking/

Drew, C. (2021, April 29). *The 4 types of critical thinking skills - Explained! (2021).* Helpful Professor. https://helpfulprofessor.com/thinking-skills/

Faber, A., & Mazlish, E. (2006). *How to talk so teens will listen and listen so teens will.* Piccadilly Press.

The history of social media: 29+ key moments. (2018, November 27). Social Media Marketing & Management Dashboard. https://blog.hootsuite.com/history-social-media/

Huang, E., CFA, & CFP®. (n.d.). *10 money management tips for teens.* Echo Wealth Management. https://www.echowealthmanagement.com/blog/10-money-management-tips-teens

Introduction to problem solving skills. (n.d.). CCMIT. https://ccmit.mit.edu/problem-solving/

Is critical thinking the same as overthinking? Some self-indulgent epistemological musings. (2019, April 25). Youth Work Hacks. https://youthworkhacks.com/is-critical-thinking-the-same-as-overthinking-some-self-indulgent-epistemological-musings/

Moore, S. (n.d.). *How to create a system that will help you with any goal.* Greatist. https://greatist.com/live/create-a-system-to-help-you-with-any-goal#1

Naik, A. (2014). *Texts, tweets, trolls and teens.* Hachette UK.

New tech northwest. (2019, August 7). New Tech Northwest – The Heart of the Northwest's Tech Community. https://www.newtechnorthwest.com/the-psychology-of-writing-down-goals/

Online safety. (n.d.). Nemours KidsHealth - the Web's most visited site about children's health. https://kidshealth.org/

en/teens/internet-safety.html

Our mission. (2014, April 11). FactCheck.org. https://www. factcheck.org/about/our-mission/

Robinson, L. (2020, January 16). *Social media and mental health.* HelpGuide.org. https://www.helpguide.org/articles/ mental-health/social-media-and-mental-health.htm

The Scientific World. (2021, March 17). *The importance of creative thinking skills in our life.* The Scientific World - Let's have a moment of science. https://www.scientificworldinfo. com/2021/03/importance-of-creative-thinking-in-life.html

Tips for safe social networking for teens. (2020, August 17). ConnectSafely. https://www.connectsafely.org/social-web-tips-for-teens/

(2018, February 5). Verywell Mind. https://www. verywellmind.com/

What is time management?: Working smarter to enhance productivity. (n.d.). Management Training and Leadership Training - Online. https://www.mindtools.com/pages/article/ newHTE_00.htm

What's the difference between social media and social networking? (n.d.). SearchUnifiedCommunications. https:// searchunifiedcommunications.techtarget.com/answer/ Whats-the-difference-between-social-media-and-social-networking

Made in United States
North Haven, CT
08 April 2022

18041018R00081